Wisconsin
SUPPER CLUBS

Wisconsin SUPPER CLUBS

AN OLD-FASHIONED EXPERIENCE

RON FAIOLA

MIDWAY

AN AGATE IMPRINT

CHICAGO

Photographs copyright © 2013 by Ron Faiola. All rights reserved.
Design by Brandtner Design

Printed in the United States of America.

Library of Congress Cataloging-in-Publication Data

Faiola, Ron.
Wisconsin supper clubs : an old-fashioned experience / by Ron Faiola.
    pages cm
Includes index.
Summary: "A guide to the supper clubs of Wisconsin"--Provided by publisher.
ISBN 978-1-57284-142-0 (hardcover) -- ISBN 1-57284-142-7 (hardcover)
1. Restaurants--Wisconsin--Guidebooks. I. Title.
TX907.3.W6F35 2013
647.957504--dc23
                    2012042650

10 9 8 7 6 5 4 3   13 14 15 16 17

Midway is an imprint of Agate Publishing. Agate books are available in bulk at discount prices. For more information, go to agatepublishing.com.

For Remy
I miss you so very much

Table of Contents

Foreword

This book is the result of of the second road trip I took to sample Wisconsin's supper clubs. The first was for my documentary, *Wisconsin Supper Clubs: An Old Fashioned Experience*, which was released in 2011 and has aired on PBS stations nationwide. The film focuses on 14 clubs around the state and has been a hit with supper club fans everywhere, especially in Wisconsin, Illinois, and the Denver area, where the film aired multiple times. When I returned to the road for this book, I learned that groups of people were following in my footsteps, going from club to club along the path I traveled in the film. During my visit to the Buckhorn, I met a couple from Springfield, Illinois, who had been to five clubs that week. On another occasion, I learned of a group of 98 people inspired by the movie had traveled in buses

from Madison to the High Shores Supper Club in Chippewa Falls, for supper and a champagne cruise (on 14 pontoon boats!).

Needless to say, I found the film's influence truly amazing. It's gratifying to know that the supper clubs are doing well, and that people are enjoying the movie and some great meals, too.

It took several weeks to visit the fifty supper clubs featured in this book. I put about 5,000 miles on my car and a few pounds around my waist along the way. While the book wasn't meant to be a review of the food, on many nights I ended up at my motel delightfully stuffed, clutching doggie bags full of leftovers.

My travels took me to big cities and small towns, along many back roads and scenic routes. I even had the hair-raising experience of driving into a raging Lake Superior storm at night. The buckets of rain pounding the windshield made it nearly impossible to see the road, let alone find my motel for the night.

Along the way, I visited Iowa, Minnesota, and Michigan's Upper Peninsula, where I immediately made a beeline for the nearest pasty shop. There's

nothing like that delicious meat-and-potato-filled treat that's unique to "da U.P.," as they say up there.

In addition to pasties and traditional supper club meals, I got to try some dishes for the first time, including frog legs (very good), chicken gizzards (yikes), alligator balls (don't ask), and deep-fried turtle fresh from the Mississippi River, which was quite tasty.

I made sure to order a brandy old-fashioned sweet—a supper club staple—at just about every club I visited. Each club prepared the drink a little differently. Some were hand muddled, some were made with a special old-fashioned mix, some were made with soda, and one was made with Southern Comfort. The garnishes varied from the traditional orange and cherry to pickled mushrooms, green olives, asparagus, and even a pickle!

I have many great memories of being on the road. I lost my way more than a few times, I occasionally grew tired of the constant travel, and I suffered a few comically frustrating motel moments. But in the end, it was a grand adventure I'll never forget.

—*Ron Faiola*

Wisconsin

SUPPER CLUBS

NORTHWEST

NORTH CENTRAL

NORTHEAST

SOUTHWEST

SOUTHEAST

N
W · E
S

Introduction

Whenever I mention that I've been to over fifty Wisconsin supper clubs, people tell me the name of their favorite club and ask if I've been there. It often turns out that I haven't. But I see that as a good thing, because it means that despite some closings, the state is full of supper clubs. How many? It's hard to tell because many of the clubs are under the radar—on rarely traveled roads, beside hidden lakes, or tucked away in tiny towns. Some can be found on the Internet, via their websites or Facebook, Yelp, and TripAdvisor, but the listings are not always comprehensive or up to date. Certain parts of the state are loaded with supper clubs. The Arbor Vitae/Woodruff area, known as the "Crossroads of the North," should really be called the "Crossroads of the Northern Supper Clubs." It has more than 20 clubs within a 30-mile radius.

Introduction

Then there's the Holyland, an area that includes portions of Fond du Lac, Calumet, and Sheboygan counties, east of Lake Winnebago. There, the area's ubiquitous Catholic churches are matched only by the numerous supper clubs. The Rock River area boasts a supper club bonanza from Watertown to Beloit, and another hot spot lies in the southwestern corner of the state, from Hazel Green north to La Crosse.

Wisconsin supper clubs originated more than eighty years ago. Many began as dance halls, taverns, roadhouses, and recreation areas. During Prohibition, some were speakeasies, and many had on-site or nearby brothels and gambling rooms. Many suffered devastating fires over the years, and were rebuilt with more space to serve the growing customer base. However, the most common trait among supper clubs is that they are family-owned, and the family usually lives on the premises.

In the early days, the menu staples were fried chicken or perch, both of which were cheap and abundant, and usually served all-you-can-eat style. By the late 1940s and early 1950s people in the United States enjoyed a higher standard of living, and these former dance halls and taverns were reborn as supper clubs. The clubs were a destination for drinks, food, and entertainment. Supper clubs welcomed everyone, no membership required.

The atmosphere at a supper club is more upscale than a tavern, and you'll usually find well-appointed table settings. There are special meals seldom found in the home kitchen: lobster, shrimp, prime rib, steak, and fish fry. Portions are big, and soups, salad dressings, and desserts are made from scratch, usually from family recipes passed down from generation to generation.

Wisconsin's affinity for brandy may have begun in supper clubs, where the brandy old-fashioned sweet is the cocktail of choice. There's also the perfect brandy Manhattan (said to have been invented at the Sky Club in Plover), plus martinis and fancy after-dinner ice cream drinks like grasshoppers and pink squirrels.

The golden age of Wisconsin supper clubs was in the 1950s and 1960s, when there was little, if any, competition from chain restaurants. Back then, supper club customers spent more time at the bar before and after a meal. When Wisconsin began to enact tougher drunk-driving laws, the supper clubs' bar business decreased. Consequently, some supper clubs—mainly in urban areas—began serving lunch to compete with the chain restaurants. (The clubs in this book only serve supper, with the exception of a few that serve Sunday brunch.)

Today, supper clubs seem to be enjoying a resurgence, as people ditch the chains in favor of the unique atmosphere, casual upscale dining, and scenic views that supper clubs offer. Some high-profile chefs in New York and Chicago are even experimenting with Wisconsin-style supper clubs. Another good sign is that the Bartolotta Group in Milwaukee is opening two supper club-style restaurants in the suburbs. I'll have to pay them a visit.

WHAT DEFINES A WISCONSIN-STYLE SUPPER CLUB? I received a list of Supper Club Selection Rules from a group of friends that frequent supper clubs on a regular basis (shown at left; you'll read more about them on page 78):

1   Prime rib or surf and turf specials every Saturday night

2   Pre-supper relish tray (preferably served on stainless steel)

3   Christmas lights strung across log structures year-round

4   Manhattans and old-fashioned cocktails automatically served with brandy

5   Waitresses that call you "Hon"

6   Jell-O served as a salad option

7   Walleye is a regular menu item

8   No cappuccino, ever

9   All-you-can-eat fried fish on Fridays

10 Grasshopper and pink Cadillac cocktails that are large enough to share

Trump Card

If there's a musical trio in the bar that knows how to play "The Girl from Ipanema," then it has to be a supper club.

Southeast Wisconsin
SUPPER CLUBS

THE MOST POPULATED AREA OF THE STATE OF WISCONSIN includes metropolitan Milwaukee, known by many monikers—the City of Festivals, Cream City, and Brew City, among others. This region includes the Horicon National Wildlife Refuge, the Basilica at Holy Hill, the Lake Country area to the west, and Lake Geneva to the south. The iconic Milwaukee Art Museum (left) overlooks the Lake Michigan shoreline, and the many recreational activities available along the shoreline include swimming, fishing, and boating.

15

COPPER DOCK *Hubertus*

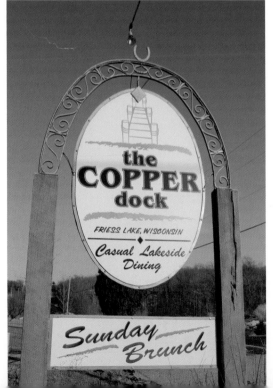

The Copper Dock is in Hubertus on the eastern shore of Friess Lake, near the Basilica at Holy Hill. Friess Lake is small—only 120 acres—but deep, with a maximum depth of 58 feet. The lake is surrounded by winding roads and hills dotted with houses.

The building that houses the Copper Dock was built in the 1930s as a resort and ice cream stand that attracted visitors from the lake's public beach. It also may have been a speakeasy and dance hall, as evidenced by the secret door buzzer behind the bar and the dance floor that remains in the bar's small dining room.

Bottom left: Owners Tim and Heather Leffler; pan-seared walleye with chive butter, green beans, and brown rice.

The original owners were the Friess family, who ran the Friess Lake Resort for three decades. They sold the business to the Anderson family, who ran the club under the name Anderson's on the Lake from 1974 until 2002, when they sold it to Tim and Heather Leffler.

The name Copper Dock came about when Tim and Heather were looking to buy the property. It was a summer evening, and as the sun was setting over the lake, it caused a reflection that Tim saw as a gleaming copper line—a copper dock.

As with most supper clubs, there is living space above the dining room, and Tim and Heather lived there with their daughter Maggie, son Max, and dog Rocco for eight years before moving to a house nearby. The apartment now houses two of their chefs.

Heather enjoyed living upstairs, but Rocco had a frustrating time smelling the delicious bacon, sausage, and roast beef during the summertime brunches on the outdoor deck. Rocco would make sad faces in the window, and customers would beg to have him come down for a treat.

When customers enter the bar area, they are heartily greeted—usually by name—by either Tim or Heather.

17

"We feel like we're inviting people into our family room, because this is our house—especially when we were living upstairs," Heather said.

When the Lefflers purchased the club from the Andersons, some people worried that the young couple would change it. "People thought we were going to be a biker bar, or we'd put in condos," Tim recalled. "But we really wanted to continue with the traditional supper club atmosphere."

One thing they did change was the menu. The couple tried fancier dishes, "with dollops of sauce here and there," according to Heather. They soon learned that the customers didn't want that. When they returned to the supper club basics—steaks, seafood, ribs and fish fry—the customers came back, and they've been doing well ever since.

One of the most popular items is the special pickled mushrooms served in the brandy old-fashioned. Tim marinates whole mushrooms in red wine vinegar, sugar, water, cinnamon, nutmeg and pickling spices. The mushrooms were so popular that Tim tried selling them in jars at Christmas one year, but now he just gives out the ingredient list for free.

The Copper Dock seats 200 people in the summer, when the outdoor deck is open, and 150 in the winter. With the huge picture windows in the dining room, there is always a wonderful view of the lake, no matter what the season. During warm weather, the club features live music on the deck, and when it's cold, the tables by the fireplace are a great place to warm up to a good meal.

Previous page: Customers Julie Halquist, Michael Batzler, and Scott Batchelor enjoy their supper. Left, from top: half rack of baby back ribs with green beans and baked potato; house salad; French onion soup; spinach salad.

My Take

During my visit to the Copper Dock, I photographed many of the club's signature dishes. While we waited for some entrées to come out of the kitchen, Tim invited me to try the soup and two salads I'd been shooting. One was the house salad with fancy mixed greens, pecans, strawberries, and lemon vinaigrette; the other was a spinach salad with hot bacon dressing. Both salads were delicious, but I think I'll always go with hot bacon dressing when it's available. The French onion soup was wonderful, capped with lots of perfectly melted cheese and a broth that had just the right saltiness.

As I was sitting at the bar enjoying the food, Tim's young daughter Maggie came in and sat down on the other side wanting some dinner. Tim asked her what she wanted, and she said, "I'll have the lamb." Tim turned to me with a look that asked, "Are you kidding me?" "See what happens when a kid grows up on supper club food?" I asked, laughing.

19

DIAMOND JIM'S STONERIDGE INN | *Hales Corners*

or those who have lived in Milwaukee for any length of time, the name "Diamond Jim" might seem familiar, whether it's for used cars (Diamond Jim's Motorcars), dirt track and jet funny car racing (Diamond Jim Racing), or fine dining and entertainment (Diamond Jim's Stoneridge Inn).

Located on a busy stretch of Janesville Road in Hales Corners, about 15 miles southwest of downtown Milwaukee, owner Jim Letizia opened Diamond Jim's Stoneridge Inn in 2001. Prior to

that, it was the Stoneridge Inn, and before that, it was the Mia Casa. In the 1970s, it was known as Larry's Steakhouse, complete with a disco, orange shag carpet on the walls, and a mirror ball hanging from the ceiling.

Today, the mirror ball and shag carpeting are gone. There are two dining rooms; one has a subtle, homey décor, and the other, which is attached to the bar, features an Italian villa theme. On Wednesdays and Saturdays, musician Red Deacon plays country music in the bar area. Red is a veteran of Milwaukee supper club entertainment who has played at the Rafters, Steakhouse 100, and Porterhouse. He's been playing supper clubs for decades, and the regulars at Diamond Jim's love him.

They also love the food. One favorite is the Chef's Choice Blue Plate Special, which varies but includes dishes like mock chicken legs prepared with chunks of veal and pork on a skewer, coated with corn flakes, pan fried, and then finished in the oven. Friday fish fry, steaks, seafood, burgers, and chicken round out the entrée menu. Suppers include a relish tray, soup or salad, choice of potato, and a fresh-baked loaf of bread.

Dean Oschmann and his wife, Dawn, are Wednesday night regulars. "My liver needs a couple of martinis, and I like to eat meat, potato, and a vegetable. That's what they serve here," Dean said, who cited meatloaf and pork schnitzel as his favorite dishes. "It's not about the $12.95—it's about what I want to eat."

Left: Supper club entertainer Red Deacon.

21

Above: Trish Lenarchich serves a brandy old-fashioned.
Next page: Relish tray and warm Italian bread; grilled
chicken, ribs, and hamburger platters.

Dean was a bartender for many years at the well-known (but now closed) Aud-Mar Supper Club on Big Muskego Lake. His family still owns the property; a proposed condo development fell through, and Dean hopes someone will reopen the supper club.

Behind the bar at Diamond Jim's stands a friendly bartender named Trish, who has worked there since 2001. She has a secret recipe for her brandy old-fashioned mix. It's so popular that she sells bottles of it at Christmas. She also helps out by making some of the homemade desserts, including cheesecake and pistachio cake.

Diamond Jim's Stoneridge Inn can seat 160 and serves 300 to 400 hungry diners during fish fry season. Sue, who is the hostess and Jim's significant other, said, "This is a special-occasion place for birthdays, anniversaries, and then we also have our regulars who come in, sometimes as often as three times per week." According to Sue, good food, good word of mouth, and Red Deacon's smooth country tunes keep them coming back.

THE DUCK INN   *Delavan*

Located on the intersection of County A and Highway 89, The Duck Inn has been open since the 1920s. During prohibition, the club was a speakeasy. In the late 1940s, according to legend, owner Freddy Adams won a large sum of money on the horses and decided to expand his supper club's bar and dining room to avoid paying taxes on his lucky windfall.

By 1986, The Duck Inn was closed. It sat unused for 8 years, until Delavan native Jeff Karbash bought it in 1994. Like Freddie Adams, Jeff also had some luck with money, although for him it was through wise stock investments and a bank that was motivated to sell. "The place was kind of a money pit because of its age," Karbash recalled. For the first five years, Karbash used the profits to maintain the property while living in the upstairs apartment.

Above: Owner Jeff Karbash
making a brandy old-fashioned.
Below: Lingonberry duck.

It's only natural that duck would be the most popular item on the menu (aside from Friday fish fry). Karbash uses farm-raised white Peking ducks, not mallards or wood ducks. He estimates that he goes through 80 ducks per week, which works out to about 200 servings, as the club serves half- and quarter-sized portions.

"Our chef, Jim, comes up with featured entrées, which are a little more exotic," Karbash said. "Some people like to experiment by trying the featured entrées, and some like to stay with the traditional items."

As with most supper clubs, everything is made from scratch, including desserts like chocolate lava cake, chocolate bourbon pecan pie, and bread pudding. Supper includes salad, choice of potato, and a cheese and cracker plate with cheddar and garlic cream cheese. A relish tray is also available for a small price. Karbash explained, "I didn't want to jack up the prices to cover the cost. I wanted to still make it available for those who want it."

Nearby lakes and campgrounds keep The Duck Inn busy during the summer, and area residents make the scenic drive out to the club the rest of the year.

Previous page: Roasted half duck jubilee.

Duck Inn Features

Appetizer - Andouille Stuffed Mushrooms

Entreés - Baked Lemon Pepper Chicken & Dumplings

Lingonberry Duck

Sesame Encrusted Salmon

Roasted Half Duck Jubilee

Potato du Jour - Carmalized Onion? Thyme?
Try a: Cha Cha Cha! Yukon Golds

ELIAS INN SUPPER CLUB *Watertown*

This small Watertown supper club attracts a huge following for its Friday fish fry. In fact, fish fry is the only "dish" available on Fridays, but it's quite a dish. Guests are given "a little bit of everything"—three pieces of fish paired with two pieces of fried chicken. The meal includes seasoned fries and a lazy susan filled with creamy potato salad, German potato salad, beans, rye bread, tartar sauce, and cole slaw.

The Elias Inn serves a traditional supper club menu the rest of the week, including a variation on the Friday night lazy susan, this time with herring, cheese spreads, sausage, cheese cubes, veggies, pickles, and pasta salad. The contents of the lazy susan itself is enough to feed a family of four.

Bottom of previous page: Owners Tammie Probst and John Elias.
Below: Owner Slim Schroeder; Watertown Mayor Ron Krueger;
original light fixture from the 1930s.

John Elias, Tammie Probst, and Greg "Slim" Schroeder opened the club in 1987. With Tammie seating guests, Slim behind the bar, and John in the kitchen, this team effort has been a successful formula for 25 years.

The Elias Inn dates back to 1933, when the building opened in downtown Watertown as Powers Inn. This tavern featured a bar complete with brass spittoons; in the back was a separate room for women. It was later renamed Wood's Old World Pub, and in 1972 a kitchen was added and it was dubbed the Watertown Inn.

The Elias Inn still contains the original bar and German-themed lighting fixtures from the 1930s. New touches have been added, including a mounted caribou, antelope, moose, buffalo, and bear. Friends of John shot some of them, a few were purchased, and the bear is "on loan," according to John.

29

"Our customers come from about a 50-mile radius," Slim said. "We seat 55 in the dining room, but we'll do about 300 fish fry dinners on Fridays." One of the club's regular customers is Watertown's mayor, Ron Krueger.

Elias doesn't take reservations, so as soon as the doors open on Fridays, the tables fill up and the dining room staff begins serving the generous portions of food to the first customers. The bar also fills quickly with guests tippling cocktails as they await a table. There's something to be said for striking up a conversation while waiting at the bar.

My Take

While I was at the bar talking with Mayor Krueger, Slim handed me a second brandy old-fashioned and informed me that my table was ready for dinner. Tammie led me into the dining room, where I sat and placed my order. I went for the "little bit of everything," plus a piece of baked cod.

Shortly after my dinner arrived, John came out to see how I like the food, and to be honest, it was outstanding. I could see why people didn't mind the wait. The fish and chicken had a light, golden breading; they were fried to perfection. The chicken was meaty and flavorful, and the both the fried and baked cod were moist and flaky. Normally I prefer my fish fry with potato pancakes, but I couldn't stop eating Elias's seasoned french fries. What a great meal in such a friendly place.

Previous page: "A little bit of everything"—chicken, fish, and fries; the Friday fish fry lazy susan. This page, from top: The weekday version of the lazy susan; baked cod; a family enjoys the Elias Inn's fish fry.

HOBNOB *Racine*

The Higgins family ran the original HobNob in downtown Racine from 1937 to 1941. After closing the restaurant during World War II, Bill Higgins Sr. opened a new HobNob in 1954 at its current location on Sheridan Road, overlooking Lake Michigan.

The building's unique design was inspired by a restaurant in California with living quarters upstairs and windows facing east and west for maximum sunlight. For years, the supper club's rooftop was used for dancing. During the '50s and '60s, the HobNob was the place to go to rub elbows with celebrities such as Roy Rogers and Dale Evans, Don Knotts, Harvey Korman, and Cloris Leachman.

The HobNob has a variety of dining rooms that can seat anywhere from 2 people to 120. The walls are adorned with unique artworks collected by Bill Higgins Jr., who took over when his father died in 1967. In the '50s and '60s the HobNob was closed every August so Bill could travel the world collecting works of art.

Current owners Mike Aletto and Anne Glowacki bought the HobNob in 1990, after

years in the hospitality industry. Mike describes the menu at the HobNob as "classic Wisconsin gourmet," with German specialties, steaks, duck, seafood, and the Flintstone steak, a huge bone-in ribeye.

On Fridays and Saturdays, the HobNob features live entertainment on the piano at the bar. "We have people in their late twenties who come in to see the restaurant of yesteryear, as well as people

celebrating their fiftieth anniversary," Mike said. He describes the look people make when they first step into the HobNob as "the blast from the past look" or "the warm, fuzzy look."

"People can count on us for a good meal," Mike said. "They're going to know we're very consistent and they feel comfortable bringing their guests here."

The HobNob sits 150 feet from the shoreline. In addition to enjoying the amazing views of Lake Michigan from the bar and restaurant, people drive down Sheridan Road to have their picture taken beside one of the "STOP LAKE MICHIGAN AHEAD" signs in the parking lot. Mike said the signs originated with the Higginses, and he's had to replace a few, but he thinks the signs were meant more as a joke than a response to any cars careening into the lake.

Clockwise from top: Thai-style duck rolls; broiled whitefish; wiener schnitzel; jumbo Gulf shrimp; filet mignon with sautéed mushrooms.

JACKSON GRILL | *Milwaukee*

Located on the corner of West Mitchell Street and South 38th Street in Milwaukee's Burnham Park neighborhood, the Jackson Grill sits about a mile south of the Miller Park baseball stadium. For 35 years, the small, two-story house was a corner tavern called Karlovitch's that served sandwiches and beer to the workers in the nearby factories. These days, the factories are gone, but the neighborhood remains working class. This low-key, friendly supper club fits right in and draws people from all over.

Heidi Schmidt and James "Jimmy" Jackson have run the Jackson Grill since it opened in 2002. It's a cozy place that includes a curved bar with about a dozen seats and a dining room that seats 35. The atmosphere at the Jackson Grill is straight out of the 1950s. Heidi's collection of vases above the bar and in the dining room provides splashes of color.

Left: A sample of the three dozen celebrity signatures on the bar's walls. Below: Bartender Alina Kubicki serves up a brandy old-fashioned; some of Heidi Schmidt's colorful vases and glass sculptures.

Signatures of celebrities hang on the walls in the bar; some are current and some date back to Jimmy's father's restaurant, which was known as Ray Jackson's Restaurant. His dad's place was located north of the old Milwaukee County Stadium on Bluemound Road.

Jimmy began his cooking career at Ray Jackson's. He then established a reputation at a number of Milwaukee's top restaurants, and, recently, he celebrated cooking his one millionth steak. Jimmy often comes out of the kitchen to greet diners and make sure they are enjoying their meals.

Heidi worked in the hospitality industry in Milwaukee before opening Jackson Grill, and she uses her experience to keep everything running smoothly. She works the front of the house, helps out at the bar, serves orders, and makes sure customers are well cared for.

With the restaurant so close to the ballpark, on game nights it's not unusual to see Cubs and Brewers fans enjoying a peaceful meal together before the game. The restaurant occasionally hosts such sports celebrities as ex-Green Bay Packers Jerry Kramer and Paul Hornung, and Brewers

announcer Bob Uecker. Major League Baseball Commissioner Bud Selig visits regularly and has a favorite table in the dining room, Jimmy said.

The menu includes a large selection of steaks, including a 32-ounce porterhouse, a bone-in ribeye, a flatiron dubbed the Jackson Grill Saloon Steak, a filet mignon, a New York strip, and an American Kobe tenderloin. Other dishes include scallops, shrimp, mahi mahi, ribs, and pastas. In the summer, guests can sit on the back patio, which also features a wood-fired oven for cooking pizza.

The Jackson Grill has the friendly atmosphere of a comfortable living room, and everyone is welcomed with a smile. When the night's cooking draws to a close, Jimmy appears from the kitchen to have a beer at the bar and chat with customers. In addition to the usual selection of specialty cocktails, the bar features the signature Jackson Grill Snifter, a custom blend of five liquors. It's especially popular during the holidays and when the weather is cold.

My Take

The Jackson Grill is just a short drive from my house. Every time I stop by, whether it's just to say hello or to have dinner, Heidi always pours me a beer at the bar and we chat. Jimmy comes out to talk for a bit before the club gets busy. After I've had a couple of beers, Heidi often asks if I'm hungry and then brings over an appetizer for me to try. Whether it's a delicious bowl of crab bisque, the sensational Cajun BBQ shrimp, or the escargots with toast and baked garlic cloves (a new favorite), it's always a wonderful treat.

I've had supper at the Jackson Grill a number of times. The seared sea scallops with saffron risotto, grilled asparagus, and tomato and tarragon sauce is delightful; the American Kobe tenderloin is one of the best and most tender steaks I've ever had. The filet with portobello mushroom cap is stellar, and the macaroni and cheese side is so good that it alone is reason enough to stop for a visit.

Above: Co-owner Heidi Schmidt.
Next page: Seared scallops; Cajun BBQ shrimp cocktail; co-owner Jimmy Jackson shows off the many cuts of meat on the menu.

Southwest Wisconsin
SUPPER CLUBS

THE LANDSCAPE OF SOUTHWESTERN WISCONSIN varies from low-lying farmland to sandstone rock formations to hillside forests and underground caves. The State Capitol in Madison lies to the east, not far from attractions such as Cave of the Mounds, Little Norway, the friendly Trolls of Mt. Horeb, and the town of Monroe, known as the "Swiss Cheese Capital of the USA." Heading north from Madison you arrive at the Wisconsin Dells, featuring rides, gambling, and other tourist attractions. To the northwest is the Driftless area, untouched by glaciers and home to the Kickapoo Indian Caverns, vineyards, and apple orchards.

3 MILE HOUSE   *Hazel Green*

What began as a supper club called the Hi Hat Club (see postcard) became the 3 Mile House in 1944, after a fire destroyed the Hi Hat Club. The new supper club got its name because it was just three miles from the Illinois border. Paul and Velma Moor purchased the 3 Mile House in 1980 and sold it to their son Jeff and daughter-in-law Julie in 1997.

Jeff and Julie have worked at the 3 Mile House since the day it opened. Jeff served drinks, cut steaks, and handled the ordering, while Julie was a waitress. After Jeff and Julie bought the supper club, Julie took over the bookkeeping, prep work, and cooking. (She also works part time at a local hospital.) Jeff and Julie raised four children—Paul, Dustin, Allie, and Hillary—in the house next door to the supper club. Today, Allie, Hillary, and Dustin still work at the 3 Mile House alongside Jeff and Julie.

All the steaks at the 3 Mile are cut by hand. At first, Jeff, his father Paul, and his sons Paul and Dustin handled that task, but these days, that duty falls to Jeff and Dustin alone. The menu at the 3 Mile House primarily features steaks, chicken, and seafood. Two of the more unusual items include Bowl of Steaks, which is tenderloin tips *au jus*, and Turtle, a deep-fried snapping turtle fresh from the Mississippi. It's served only on Wednesdays and Thursdays, when available. Meals at the 3 Mile come with cabbage salad, cottage cheese or tossed salad, a choice of potato or vegetable, a relish tray, cheese spread (3 Mile's own brand), crackers, and dinner rolls.

Previous page: 3 Mile House bartender Will Pearce.
Top: Original postcard of the Hi Hat Club.

Since the younger Paul was 15, he would report to the club every day after school to learn the art of bartending alongside his grandfather and father. He ended up working behind the bar for 13 years. Paul's brother Dustin is a full-time buyer at Flexsteel, but still helps out at the supper club when he can.

The busiest night ever at the 3 Mile House, according to Paul, was one New Year's Eve when the club hosted more than 475 people. "For a place that can seat 84, it was a crazy night," Paul said. According to Paul, Dustin made so many blender drinks that night he "nearly froze his hand off."

Far right: 3 Mile House owner Jeff Moor. Next page: A plastic turtle on the bar; the deep-fried turtle dinner.

Sons Paul and Dustin have considered buying the club from their parents. For now, though, they've been working on their 3 Mile House Grocery business, which began with the club's special cheese spread and now includes Braunschweiger (liverwurst) and roast beef. You can find the 3 Mile's cheese spread today at the 3 Mile and its grocery, and at 60 other grocery stores from Cedar Rapids, Iowa to Madison, Wisconsin.

My Take

When I saw deep-fried turtle on the menu, I mentioned to Jeff that I had never seen it before, let alone tried it. Before I knew it, an order was sitting on the bar for me. Bartender Will suggested I dig into one of the pieces that didn't have a bone sticking out of it, which I considered to be good advice. The turtle was deep fried in a light batter, and the meat was moist. It tasted like dark meat turkey, not gamey at all. Most important, it was delicious.

Jeff and Julie also own the Gas 'n' Moor gas station/convenience store located in front of the 3 Mile House. As I was about to leave, I mentioned to Jeff that I planned to gas up the car at their station; Jeff kindly advised me to drive across the river to Dubuque, Iowa, where the gas was about 30 cents cheaper per gallon.

He also gave me a container of their 3 Mile House Cheese Spread, "for the road." It came in handy as I headed toward my next stop, snacking on the tasty cheese along the way.

BENEDETTI'S SUPPER CLUB *Beloit*

Benedetti's Supper Club dates back to 1944, when Elmer and Tosca Benedetti opened the Yost Park Tavern. A fire destroyed the Tavern in 1946. The newly rebuilt tavern was christened Club 51 because of its location along Highway 51, between Beloit and Janesville.

After Elmer died in 1953, Tosca continued to run the bar and restaurant with the help of her son Ken and his wife, Lois. By then, Club 51 was famous for its 75-cent fish-fry dinners. Its bar was remodeled in 1955, and the occasion called for a name change, to Benedetti's Supper Club.

In 1995, Tosca's grandson Elmer and his wife, Sandy, took over the business. Elmer, a chef, would run the kitchen when he wasn't working his day job—piloting private jets. Photos on the wall in the bar show some of the jets Elmer flew, and customers often look for him when he's in town. "He's Mr. Entertainment," Sandy said.

Benedetti's is open Wednesday through Saturday, year round. Its main dining room seats 85, and the south dining room, normally reserved for the Friday fish fry or private events, holds 60. The club's busiest night is Friday, when they serve an average of 400 meals.

"We believe that business comes where it is invited and stays where it is appreciated."

The Benedettis

On Saturday, the club features prime rib; on Thursday, the crowds come in for BBQ ribs and a popular chicken and dumplings dinner; and on Wednesday, smelt and catfish are the catch of the day. Meals include a soup and salad bar except on Fridays, when Grandma Tosca's special cole slaw is the side delight.

While Elmer is flying, Sandy handles the day-to-day business operation. She's helped out by her sons Homer and Mitchell, who take turns in the kitchen. Along with the fish fry, Benedetti's is also well known for its grasshopper, which may be the largest ice cream dish in the state. "We can get four grasshoppers out of a three gallon bucket of ice cream," Sandy said. The club goes through 30 gallons of ice cream a week.

Customers come from all over: Beloit, Janesville, Rockford, Madison, and even farther. "Some customers drove down from Wausau to show their teenage daughters what a supper club was like," Sandy recalled. "They were dressed up, and got a kick out of the grasshopper."

BUCKHORN SUPPER CLUB Milton

The Buckhorn Supper Club sits on the scenic eastern shores of Lake Koshkonong, which is part of the Rock River. Although the lake covers 10,000 acres, it is relatively shallow, with an average depth of only about 6 feet. The Buckhorn was built in the early 1940s on Charley Bluff Road and named for a French fur trader who lived in the area. For about 50 years, the Buckhorn was known as a tavern that served food for the local residents who came to swim and fish in the lake.

Current owners Dawn and Chico Pope had been in the restaurant management business for many years before deciding to buy the Buckhorn in 1997. Dawn knew the club well, having gone there every weekend with her parents as a child.

Chico said, "We thought it would be a good opportunity for our children to work with us, but we didn't really expect them to be here 15 years later." Their son Kevin is now the head chef, and their daughter Shelley shares hostessing duties with Dawn.

As you walk into the Buckhorn and are greeted by the Pope family, you'd think you were walking into their home. And you'd be right—the kitchen is attached to their house. The family's back patio looks directly out onto the lake. When people find out the Popes live there, Dawn exclaims, "Welcome to my backyard!"

The Buckhorn is open Thursday through Sunday in the summer, and Friday through Sunday all winter long. "Being open three days is great," Dawn said. "People wonder what we do the rest of the time, and there is a lot of work, with deliveries and landscaping. But it's also nice to sit back, relax, and look out over the lake."

The menu at the Buckhorn offers traditional Saturday prime rib and Friday fish fry dinners, plus seafood and specialties. These include roast duck with Door County cherry glaze, BBQ ribs, broasted chicken with dumplings, and, occasionally, frog legs. Once the word gets out about the frog legs, they go quickly.

The club's popular lobster boil started off as a Door County-style fish boil. For about six years, the fish boil had intermittent success—until the switch was made from fish to lobster. The club offers the lobster boil on the last Wednesday of each month during the summer. "It's become a real nice event," said Chico. "The lobsters are flown in fresh from the Atlantic, just north of Maine. They fly them to Chicago on Tuesday night and they're delivered to the Buckhorn Wednesday morning, and we're eating them that night."

Previous page, bottom left: Owners Dawn and Chico Pop (second and fourth from left) with their children, Kevin Pope and Shelley Huhnke. Near left, from top: A "saddle" of frog legs; roast duck with Door County cherry sauce; Dawn serves up a brandy old-fashioned.

For the lobster boils, the Buckhorn receives about 90 live lobsters that range from 1 1/2 to 1 3/4 pounds. The lobsters are placed in a metal basket and are brought out to the diners, who often take photos before the basket gets dunked in the boiling water. Once in the pot, the lobsters take about 20 minutes to cook. At the end, there's a big photo-op flame-over, when Kevin tosses kerosene into the fire. Afterward, the lobsters are placed in the dining room, where they're served with drawn butter, salad, rolls, corn on the cob, potatoes, dessert, and local wine.

From top: Kevin Pope and chef Jeff Hanson lower the lobsters into the pot. Later, Kevin tosses kerosene on the fire for the big flame-over.

My Take

I've been to the Buckhorn many times, and since my first visit, I've always been treated well—almost like part of the family. Chico, Dawn, and Shelley always stop by to say hello, and even on a busy night, Kevin will pop out of the kitchen for a quick visit. The food is always wonderful, and I've tried just about everything on the menu, including the lobster boil.

Since the release of my supper club movie, the Buckhorn's lobster boils have become so popular that extra dates were added to accommodate demand. The club now sells lobster-themed caps and T-shirts emblazoned with the motto, "Come Get Some Tail."

The lobster boils are great for mixing with other patrons because everyone is having the same meal at the same time. Chico acts as MC for the evening, announcing when the lobsters are ready for photos—especially when the big flame-over is about to happen—and later welcoming everyone to sit down for dinner. It's a lot of fun. Everyone wears lobster bibs, and while getting to the lobster meat is a bit of work, it's worth every delicious, buttery bite.

After a great meal at the Buckhorn, I always have to try one of the homemade desserts. In addition to the spectacular key lime and chocolate peanut butter pies, I recently got a chance to enjoy the club's superb banana cream pie. It was so delicious that I almost forgot about how good my entrée had been.

Speaking of dessert, the Buckhorn's key lime pie and chocolate peanut butter pie are very popular and are usually made by either Dawn or Kevin. Many of the staff at the club have been around since day one, and so have many of its regular customers. Dawn said, "We have wonderful customers who come by every week, and when they don't, they call us to let us know."

Clockwise from top left: Lobster bibs at the ready; Chico Pope, Dawn Pope, Shelley Huhnke, Kevin Pope, Jane Bauer (Chico's sister), and Ron Bauer; sunset over Lake Koshkonong; prime rib; cooked lobster.

THE BUTTERFLY CLUB *Beloit*

The Butterfly Club is located on the outskirts of Beloit on County Highway X, in the little town of Turtle. The club dates back to 1924, when a couple named Hal and Mae Sherburne built the Butterfly Tea Room, complete with kitchen, bar, and three dining rooms on two levels. The name came from Mae, who noticed the many butterflies in the field near the tearoom. The butterflies had staying power, as a neighboring housing development is called Butterfly Acres.

In 1938, Benjamin Hoffman bought the business and renamed it the Butterfly Club. Eight years later, Army veteran Mike Molay took ownership, and over the next couple of decades, he added a modern cocktail lounge with entertainment and a fish fry.

In 1972, Molay's Butterfly Club was destroyed in a fire. It was rebuilt a year later and sold to the Camboni family in 1977. At that time, the club was extensively remodeled, including installation of an outdoor deck with a scenic view of the neighboring tree-covered hills.

In 1999, the business was sold again, this time to brothers Mike and Hektor Sala. Born in Albania, the Salas worked in Greece for a time before immigrating to the United States. Prior to buying the Butterfly Club, the brothers managed a restaurant in Monroe, Wisconsin. Today, six Sala family members work at the Butterfly, including Mike's wife Sonila and Hektor's wife Uljana. In total, the brothers employ 30 people at the Butterfly.

The club's dining rooms can accommodate 180, and in summer, the outside deck seats another 50. The busiest night at the Butterfly Club is Friday, when the fish fry and live music draws as many as 400 to 450 people. On Saturdays, the club serves about 250, and weekdays average about half that.

The Butterfly's menu has something for everyone, including steaks, chicken livers, walleye, prime rib, seafood, and a variation of shrimp de Jonghe (a Chicago-based dish) baked with mushrooms and onions in a puff pastry shell. Supper includes soup, salad, a potato or vegetable, and

Top left: Fresh-baked bread and sweet rolls. Above from top: Shrimp de Jonghe; cheese-topped steak with onion rings; prime rib and Honduran shrimp.

a basket of freshly baked bread, which includes sweet rolls, an item unique to Beloit-area supper clubs. The daily specials range from the "Fish Fanfare"—a standard fish fry—to baby beef livers sautéed in onions and bacon.

The Butterfly Club is a busy, spacious place with a cocktail lounge that features live music and dancing on Fridays and Saturdays. The club's food is so good that the owners of the Buckhorn in Milton often bring their own staff to dine there on special occasions.

CIMAROLI'S SUPPER CLUB *Portage*

"Out in the boonies" would be an apt description of the location of Cimaroli's, which you'll find between Portage and the Wisconsin Dells at the intersection of County Roads XX and AA. Surrounded by farm fields, the original building served as a gas station and dance hall.

Later, it was known as Ye Olde Johnson's Inn Supper Club, until Ron Cimaroli purchased it in 1970. After a devastating fire in 2005, Cimaroli's was rebuilt on a site about 100 yards from the original location. Cimaroli's today is a 21st-century supper club with modern decor.

Left: Steaks cooking on the grill.
*Below left: Bartender Johanna Weith
and former owner Ron Cimaroli.*

Thinking back to the early days of his ownership of the club, Ron recalled, "When you first open, you don't know what you're doing, but it did lock in after about four years, and it got busy after you paid your dues."

Cimaroli's is known for its flatiron steaks, which come in 5-, 10-, and 16-ounce portions, as well as its prime rib, which ranges from 6-ounce to 32-ounce cuts. The 24-ounce cut is the most popular.

Ron sold the club to his son Jamie in 2000, but Ron still comes in several nights a week. He's known as the club's beverage director and entertainer, serving drinks and playing keyboards for the bar crowd. Ron is a music veteran who once performed with with Bing Bang and the Entertainers, a band that plays a variety of early rock and easy listening tunes in area supper clubs and Hoffman House restaurants.

Today, Cimaroli's seats about 100, and the club serves about 400 to 500 meals on the weekends. Customers start lining up outside the door about 10 to 15 minutes before it opens. Ron and his fellow bartender Johanna watch to see which customers are waiting, so they can pour their drinks and place them on the bar as they enter.

Ron's philosophy is low prices, high volume, and customer service. "This is what we do for a living," he said. "If you don't want to deal with people, you shouldn't be in this business."

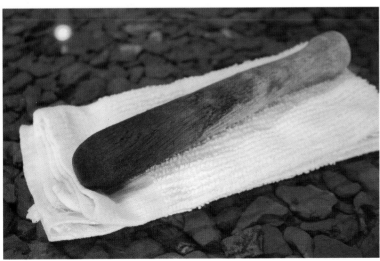

Previous page: Current owner Jamie Cimaroli
(on the right), with Tony Cimaroli in the kitchen.
Left: A muddler well worn from making brandy
old-fashioneds.

COUNTRY HEIGHTS SUPPER CLUB AND MOTEL — *Hazel Green*

Cathy Brotzman owns this combination supper club and motel with her husband, Mike. Cathy works behind the bar; Mike is the chef. They've owned the club since 1969, and the motel was added in 1986. Their house sits on the north side of the motel. "Sometimes I want to get rid of the motel; sometimes I want to get rid of the supper club," Mike said with a smile.

Business was better when the club was on the original Highway 61. Today, a new highway bypasses Country Heights, and a casino across the border in Iowa draws crowds. The extreme southwest corner of Wisconsin is interesting because of the number of supper clubs located there, including the Kall Inn, Red Top, and 3 Mile

House. Several others lie just over the border in Dubuque, Iowa, including the Moracco, Timmerman's, Rosewood, and Sweeney's. Still more are in nearby Cuba City and Dickeyville.

The place is big, with capacity to seat 250 people in the dining room and bar. Country Heights offers a large salad bar and a menu filled with steaks and seafood. Sometimes snowmobilers stop in and, misunderstanding the meaning of "supper club," ask if they have to join the club to eat there.

Top, from left: Barry Rokusek, Joyce Conner, Nate Brown, and Country Heights owner Cathy Brotzman. Above: Twice-baked potato, fried alligator, shrimp cocktail, and onion rings.

My Take

This perfect combination of supper club and motel was my final destination in Hazel Green after a long day on the road. I paid for my room at the supper club bar, unloaded the car, washed up, and headed over to the club for supper.

As I sat at the bar talking with Cathy and her friends, I decided to order a few of the club's appetizers: fried alligator, shrimp cocktail, onion rings, and a twice-baked potato. Earlier in the day, I'd had some deep-fried turtle and steak at the 3 Mile House, so the appetizers were just what I was looking for. (And how cool is it to have turtle and alligator in one day?)

After the kitchen closed, I stayed at the bar for a while talking with Mike and Cathy. A couple more beers and then it was time to stroll back to the motel and go to bed. In the simple but well-appointed motel room, I dreamed of moving in—there's nothing like a nice room with a supper club just steps away.

DING-A-LING SUPPER CLUB   *Hanover*

K nown as the Ding-A-Ling since the 1940s, this Hanover supper club is actually the second of a pair of clubs. The original family that owned the clubs opened the first location in Mercer, where it remains open to this day. Later, the owners opened a new Ding-A-Ling in Hanover and moved there as well. The family lived in a back room, which today is a dining room. As the Hanover location grew in popularity, an additional dining room just off the bar was added in the 1960s.

In 2006, current owners Kyla and Jerrad Wilke bought the club from Merrill and Marianne Perius, who had owned it for more than 25 years. Kyla had worked for Merrill and Marianne as a bartender and hostess for four years before buying the club, but Marianne stayed on for six months to help the Wilkes learn the business.

"I'm not in this business to get rich," Kyla said. "To keep people coming back, you've got to keep the prices down [and] serve good food at good prices."

From top: Outside the Ding-A-Ling; customers at the bar; owner Kyla Wilke serving a drink; fried chicken dinners with mashed potatoes and gravy.

The drive to the Ding-A-Ling is scenic and remote, but it's really not that far from Janesville. The supper club draws a loyal crowd of diners young and old, as its parking lot is always full of everything from motorcycles to SUVs. The place is small, so the wait for a table can be long.

"One night we had a three-and-a-half-hour wait, and people didn't mind!" Kyla recalled. "It's been a very popular place—I can't figure it out. We're very lucky."

One reason might be chef Carlos Dimas, who has been cooking at the Ding-A-Ling for the last 15 years. The menu offers steak, seafood, and an all-you-can-eat fish fry, along with surf and turf specials, fajitas, stir fry, and chicken with dumplings.

The Ding-A-Ling is surrounded by acres of farm fields. Kyla said that neighboring farmers come here for a "big chunk of meat and potato."

Jerrad is a partial owner, of course, but he works full time on his father's dairy farm raising beef cows and crops. Kyla runs the supper club. Jerrad occasionally brings their two children (a third is on the way) to eat at the Ding-A-Ling, but the Wilkes are glad to work their separate jobs. As Kyla put it, "I don't want to work with my husband. I'd rather be married to him!"

DORF HAUS | *Roxbury/Sauk City*

Visitors experience a taste of Germany at the Dorf Haus. German specialties and live Bavarian music are served up Wednesday through Sunday in Roxbury, just south of Sauk City and 24 miles northwest of Madison. The Dorf Haus was originally opened in 1959 by Vern and Betty Maier. It gained popularity with an all-you-can-eat chicken and fish dinner for one dollar. Back then, people would stand in line with plastic numbers, waiting for their meals.

The club's name means "village house" or "small village inn," but there's nothing small about the Dorf Haus. The club offers seating for over 200, including a large banquet hall complete with a stage for dinner theater performances and weddings. "We do 40 weddings per year," said Rebecca Maier-Frey (daughter of Vern and Betty), who runs the Dorf Haus with her brother Monte Maier.

Bavarian Smorgasbord

Includes salad bar and dessert.
First Monday of every month year round. First and third Monday June - October.

LIVE OOMPAH MUSIC!

Knackwurst	Weiner Schnitzel	Hocks	Nudeln
Schweinsrippen	Pork Schnitzel	Späetzle	Kraut
Sauerbraten		Kartoffel	

Speisekarte
German Specialties

Haus specialties include soup and salad bar.

Wiener Schnitzel
Tender veal cutlets breaded and pan fried till golden brown, accompanied with flour dumplings - 17.95

Jäger Schnitzel
"Hunters Schnitzel." Tender breaded veal cutlets, pan fried, topped with a delectable mushroom sauce and served with flour dumplings - 18.95

Rahmschnitzel
Lightly breaded pork cutlets, served with a luscious cream sauce and choice of potato - 15.95

Sauerbraten
Marinated beef covered with our special ginger snap sauce. Served over our haus recipe späetzle and accompanied with red cabbage - 15.95

Schweinsbraten
A specially selected pork shank, richly flavored when baked. Served with sauerkraut, apple sauce and potato - 16.95

German Combination
"Best of the wurst and a hock." Knackwurst, Weisswurst and a smoked pork hock. Served with German potato salad and red cabbage - 15.95

Kassler Rippchen
Tender, lightly smoked thick cut pork chop complimented with sauerkraut, apple sauce and potato - 13.95

Rouladen
U.S.D.A. Beef sliced and topped with bacon, onion and pickle, then rolled and baked till tender in a delicious mushroom gravy. Served with red cabbage and choice of potato - 15.95

■ Haus Specialty

Monte has been working at the supper club since 1976, and Rebecca since 1992. It's a true family business: Rebecca's oldest child is 12 and can't wait to start to working at the Dorf Haus.

Today, the Dorf Haus menu ranges from traditional supper club fare to German dishes of wiener schnitzel, sauerbraten, rouladen, and pork shoulder. The club's fish fry is served family style, all-you-can-eat, and has been voted the second-best Madison-area fish fry. That's quite an accomplishment, considering that the Dorf Haus is more than 20 miles from the capital.

71

Dorf Haus

Serving Hours

Wed - Thurs 5:00 pm to 8:30 pm
Fri - Sat...... 5:00 pm to 10:00 pm
Sun...........11:30 am to 8:30 pm

Bavarian Smorgasboard

1st Mon each month all year
1st and 3rd Mon, June - Oct. from 5-9 p.m.

Suppers are served with the Maiers' grandmother's fritters, made with a sweetened bread dough. There's also a salad bar featuring pickled chicken gizzards, beets, cottage cheese, macaroni salad, bean salad, liver pâté, and cheddar cheese spread. The soup of the day is always chicken dumpling, and dinners include a choice of potatoes, flour dumplings, or spaetzle.

The Dorf Haus features dinner-theater nights and a 16-piece Bavarian band in the fall. The wait for a table, especially on Fridays, can range from one to two hours, but guests can pass the time with a German beer at the bar. There's also a game room for kids and a pool table for adults.

"We're 20 minutes from anywhere," said Rebecca. "We're a destination for people to come here and relax or come for the experience."

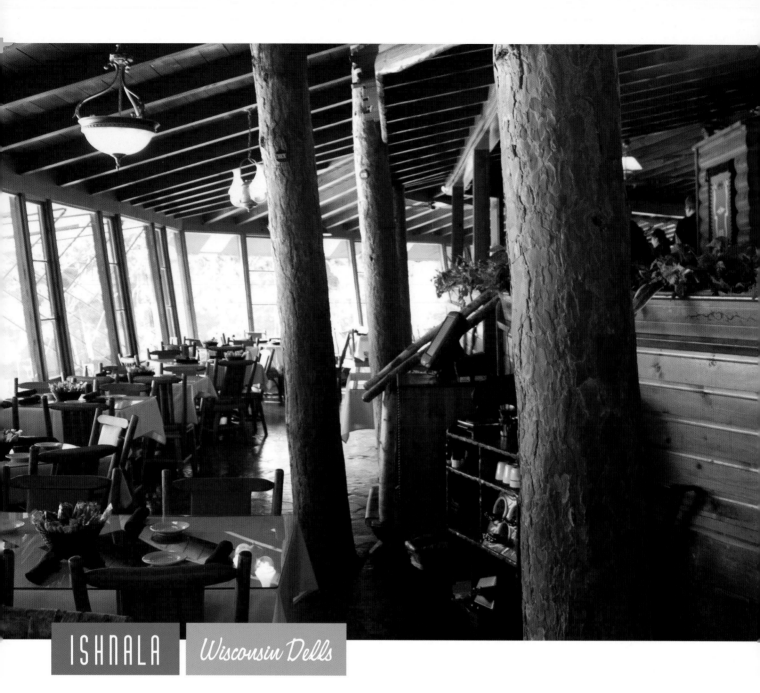

ISHNALA | *Wisconsin Dells*

Overlooking Mirror Lake and surrounded by Mirror Lake State Park, Ishnala is one of the most unique, well known, and scenic supper clubs in the state. The word "Ishnala" means "by itself alone," and it began as a Native American trading post in the late 1800s. In the early 1900s, the Coleman family bought the property and turned it into a private residence. Both the original trading post and the Coleman family home remain part of the building today.

In 1953, the property was purchased by the seven Hoffman brothers, the same brothers who started the popular Hoffman House restaurant chain after returning from military service in 1946. The brothers added 100 tons of flagstone to support a dining room, an arrowhead-shaped bar (appropriately called Arrowhead Bar), and outdoor decks. The construction of the dining room included building around several live pine trees. To this day, those same pine trees continue to grow inside Ishnala, and each is named after one of the brothers.

In addition to the scenic views of the lake, there is much to see inside and out at Ishnala. Stuffed and mounted animals gaze out from the walls, and Chief Ishnala stands guard by the bar. On the grounds by the main entrance sits a century-old canoe made from a tree trunk; the canoe was found at the bottom of Mirror Lake. Lining the walkway that leads to Ishnala are a gift shop and a small teepee, which overlooks the lake. The teepee is a popular destination for souvenir photographs. Tiki torches mark the way down the path from the parking lot to the entrance. The winding road that

Far right: Chief Ishnala wearing a sign that reads, "Bonjau Nitchie," meaning "Good Day, Friend." Next page: Pathway from the parking lot; sunset over Mirror Lake; dinners of roast Wisconsin duck and filet with twin lobsters.

My Take

As I was on the road writing this book, I received an email from Tim Dodge, who is part of a longstanding group of supper club aficionados. I decided to meet the group at Ishnala shortly after it opened for the season.

We met at the Arrowhead Bar around 7 p.m. The group included four Milwaukee-area couples: Tony and Vicki Kunz, Tim and Denise Dodge, Rich and Kimberly Lock, and Katy and Jim Young.

After enjoying a couple of cocktails, we sat down for supper. I asked Tim about his group, and he said, "Our [dinner group] was born out of pure desperation. There were always excuses for why we couldn't get together with friends. Then Jim and Katy came up with an idea. What if we made a standing night out together on the first Friday of every month? And what if, each month, we visited a different Wisconsin supper club?"

Ten years later, they're still hitting the supper clubs together. This night was a first time at Ishnala for some of the group, so Bob Prosser made sure we were seated by a window. In between the appetizers, salads, and entrées, we talked about food, supper clubs, and the group's supper club experiences over the years. Jim Young pulled out a notebook and began to read hilarious reviews of past supper club meetings.

A few ice cream drinks and coffee ended the night. Our group was the last to leave Ishnala, but not before taking a few more photos and saying some long goodbyes.

Looking back on the evening, I recalled something Tim had said about the group. "We enjoy remembering the simpler time of the generations that went before us. A time and place when going out wasn't about being hip, and the food being served was less important than the laughter and the stories and the friends whom you shared it with." Indeed.

leads to Ishnala was made famous in the Johnny Depp movie "Public Enemies." The road appears in the scene where the FBI raids Little Bohemia and John Dillinger (Depp) makes his escape.

Overseeing operations at Ishnala today is Bob Prosser. He started his career with the Hoffman brothers in 1973, as a bus boy at a Wausau Hoffman House, and became the company's president in 1999. His daughter Jamie waits tables at the club while she attends college.

Ishnala can seat 160 people, and with two levels of seating, pretty much everyone gets a lovely view of the lake. On a busy night, the club serves 500 to 600 meals. Much like the rest of the Dells area, Ishnala is seasonal, open seven nights a week from May to October.

Previous page, from top: Filet with twin lobsters; fried cheese curds; bruschetta. Above: Patron Tim Dodge (far right) and his supper club group toast to another good meal.

JONES' BLACK ANGUS | *Prairie du Chien*

Steve and Angie Jones purchased this popular Prairie du Chien supper club from the Jeffers family in 2007. Steve and Angie hail from Prairie du Chien, and they happened to visiting the club for a cocktail when they heard the place was for sale. With some savings and a bit of luck, they reopened the club as Jones' Black Angus. "We tweaked the menu a bit, but basically kept it the same," Steve said.

The club's history dates back to 1940, when Lawrence and Loretta Geisler built a roadhouse on the outskirts of Prairie du Chien. Five years later, the Geislers moved the business downtown to a site on Blackhawk Avenue, and it became known as Geisler's Corner. The space was later sold to an employee, George Jeffers, and his wife Dorothy, and the couple renamed it Jeffers' Nite Club. The club burned to the ground in 1965, but it was rebuilt as Jeffers' Black Angus at its current location.

George and Dorothy's daughter Ginger and her husband Zeke bought the business in 1978 and kept the name Jeffers' Black Angus. The couple did some major remodeling in 1988, adding a lounge in the bar area and expanding the dining room. In April 1998, Bob and Sheri Kenneth assumed ownership and changed the name to The Angus. In 2004, Ginger and Zeke repurchased the club and restored the Jeffers' Black Angus name. Today, under Steve and Angie's ownership, Jones'

Previous page: Chef Jim Weaver at work.
Right: Surf and turf with cheese-covered hash browns.

Black Angus serves about 250 to 300 dinners on weekends, and also hosts wedding banquets and other private parties. A couple recently celebrated their fiftieth anniversary party there because they'd held their wedding reception at the Black Angus.

The club's steaks range from the popular tenderloin filet to a massive bone-in ribeye called the Tomahawk. Chef Jim Weaver grills steaks, fries hash browns, and sautées vegetables on a broiler in the dining room, so customers can come up and watch him work.

Bottom of previous page: Owners
Steve and Angie Jones at the bar.
Above: Grasshopper, martini, and
brandy old-fashioned.

My Take

Before leaving Prairie du Chien for my next stop, I visited the Lady Luck Casino. The casino's mascot is a 50-year-old statue of a pink elephant wearing a top hat. Cleverly named Pinky, the coral-colored pachyderm used to welcome customers to The Pink Elephant Supper Club, which sat on the Lady Luck's site. Pinky turned out to be a lucky charm for me, as I ended up winning a sizable sum on a slot machine inside the casino a few minutes later. Thanks, Pinky!

Besides steaks, the Black Angus also offers several seafood selections, and a large soup and salad bar and a freshly baked loaf of bread comes with every meal. The fried cheese curds, a very popular appetizer, are pieces of locally sourced, battered white cheddar that are served hot from the fryer.

Just across the Mississippi River, in Marquette, Iowa, lies the Lady Luck casino. In earlier days, the casino sent high rollers to the Black Angus for free lobster and steak dinners. Even though those days are over, Steve said that the casino is still good for their business, as gamblers often like to treat themselves to a nice meal after winning some money.

Patrons of the supper club include the young and old, regular customers and tourists. Fall is the club's busiest time, Angie, said, because of the "leaf-lookers."

"The only thing predictable about the restaurant business is that it's unpredictable," Angie said.

LIBERTY INN | *Beloit*

S ituated in a suburban neighborhood along Highway 81, just west of downtown Beloit, the Liberty Inn began as a chicken hatchery in the 1920s. The business didn't change hands until 1974, when it became Larry's Supper Club. It later changed owners again and became the Liberty Inn.

Next page, top right: Owner Casey Singles enjoying a cocktail at the bar with his customers. Next page, bottom right: Apple-and-walnut-stuffed pork loin with a cranberry apple reduction.

Chef Features

Flatbread Pizza: Cheese & Sausage 6.95
            Chicken & Artichoke 7.95
            Vegetarian 6.95

Chef's Beef Tips with Shrimp & 23.95
Gnocchi Pasta & Garlic Chili Sauce

Apple & Walnut Stuffed Pork Loin & 22.95
with Cranberry Apple Reduction

Spinach & Tomato Filled Trout with 24.95
Wild Rice & Vermouth Pan Sauce

Welcome BIFF Attndees

Current owner Casey Singles bought the Liberty Inn in 2005. Previously, he'd owned another legendary Beloit supper club, the Gun Club, for more than a decade. The Gun Club burned to the ground in 2010, long after he'd sold it, but Casey was heartbroken to see it go up in flames. "A good part of my life was spent there," explained Casey.

The Liberty Inn's menu features prime rib, steaks, chops, and seafood. It also offers a variety of upscale, yet reasonably priced, chef specials, including shepherd's pie, beef Wellington, sautéed frog legs, red snapper, catfish, trout, and ahi tuna. "I like to get good seafood and let my chefs prepare it appropriately," Casey said.

Chef's beef tips with shrimp and gnocchi pasta and garlic aioli sauce; apple-and-walnut-stuffed pork loin with a cranberry apple reduction; trout baked with spinach and tomato, served in a vermouth pan sauce alongside wild rice.

The main dining room can seat about 40 and the bar has room for 15 to 20. There's additional seating downstairs in a banquet room, which also has a bar that's decorated with a golf theme. In the dining room bar hangs the original windows from the front of the chicken hatchery building. Casey found them in storage after he bought the club and decided to use them as part of the wall that divides the bar and dining room.

Casey is a friendly, down-to-earth character. After he finishes getting the club ready to open, he can usually be found behind the bar serving drinks and entertaining customers with his usual cheerful demeanor.

My Take

My film, *Wisconsin Supper Clubs: An Old Fashioned Experience,* was shown at the 2012 Beloit International Film Festival (BIFF). On the opening night of the festival, Casey held a private party at the Liberty Inn for BIFF's filmmakers and organizers.

The party was held in the inn's downstairs banquet room. Casey turned the party into a showcase for Wisconsin culture and products, as many of the other filmmakers were from other states and even other countries. In addition to screening my movie, Casey made his Friday fish fry and served a variety of Wisconsin cheese, beer, and wine for the guests.

The party was a huge success. The club was packed with people enjoying the movie and sampling Wisconsin food and drinks. Casey made sure it was a special night.

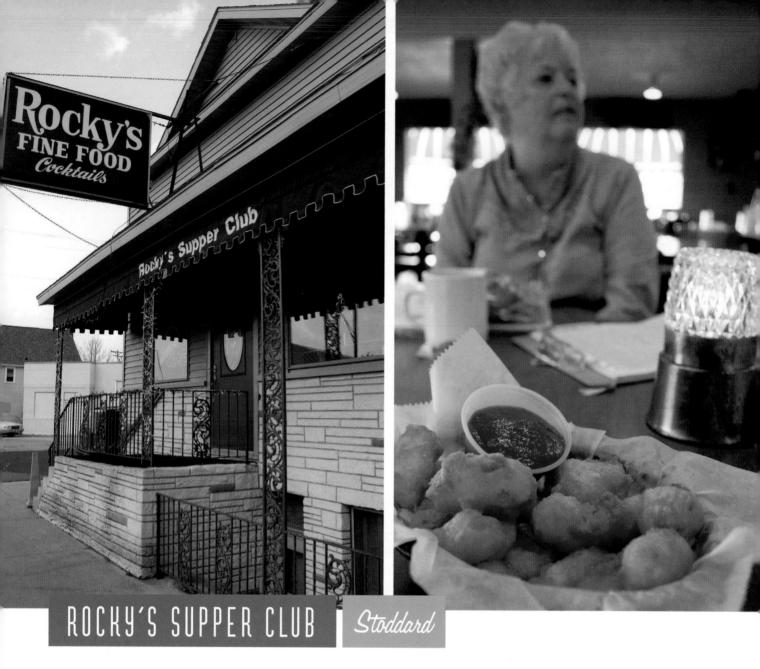

ROCKY'S SUPPER CLUB | *Stoddard*

The town of Stoddard, population 779, sits beside the Mississippi River on the Great River Road, which is also known as Highway 35 and, in Stoddard, Main Street. The town boasts spectacular views of towering sandstone bluffs on both banks of the river. Rocky's Supper Club is conveniently located on Main Street in the heart of Stoddard. There's a tavern across the street, and the post office is a half block north. A few houses sit on either side of the street. It'd be easy to rumble right through Stoddard without stopping, if not for Rocky's Supper Club.

The building that currently houses Rocky's began as the Hotel Wodzynsky in 1895. In the 1950s, Earl and Ione Pennel, who were known as "Rocky" and "Toots," respectively, bought the hotel and added a bar dubbed Rocky's Tavern. In 1959, they added a kitchen and rechristened the business Rocky's Supper Club.

Rocky's was purchased by Janet Stearns and her husband Norm in 1972. Since the Stearns didn't have any restaurant experience, Rocky and Toots stuck around to teach them the business. The Stearns lived above the dining room, and Janet still lives there to this day. Janet and her daughter Jaynne Lepke recently celebrated the 40th anniversary of their ownership of Rocky's with a four-day party that featured bands and special "retro" menu prices.

Previous page: Cheese curds with co-owner Janet Stearns in background. Above: Baked fish; relish trays.

Rocky's is known far and wide for two items: handmade fried cheese curds and special bleu cheese dressing, which is served on both the baked cod and burgers. Rocky's bleu cheese blend is so popular that the club sells to-go containers of it. One customer from Minnesota liked the dressing so much that she bought nine containers of it for the road. Janet's fried cheese curds are so legendary that at the town's annual Riverfest celebration, she's known to all as the "Cheese Curd Lady." "During the five days of Riverfest, we'll sell two tons of fried cheese curds," Jaynne said.

Janet claims to have originated the battered fried cheese curds in the '70s. "There was a local creamery, and they were giving the curds away back then. They aren't now," she said with a wink.

What make her curds unique are the secret ingredients in the batter, which she won't divulge.

Besides the fried cheese curds, one of the main reasons that people keep coming back to Rocky's is its chef, Mark Peterson, who has been cooking there for 32 years. He's known for his specials: In addition to the fish fry, steaks, and seafood, Mark likes to feature Mexican dishes on Thursdays. On Friday nights, Rocky's serves about 300 fish fry dinners.

Jaynne works the bar, serves meals, and greets the guests with a friendly smile. As she surveyed the busy supper club on the night I visited, she remarked, "The best part about the supper club thing is community. This is a place for the community to gather; we know our customers, they know us, and they know each other."

My Take

When I sat down with Janet for an interview, the topic of fried cheese curds came up quickly. Janet said, "I've got them working on an order for you!" Sure enough, a few minutes later, a basket full of battered curds, hot from the fryer, were placed in front of me, with some seafood sauce on the side. I picked out one of the bigger pieces, popped it in my mouth, and thought, "Yep, these are great, no need to dip them in anything." The secret batter and the creamy saltiness of the cheese combine to make the perfect fried curd.

Janet sat beside me with a smile, watching me enjoy the curds. After I'd eaten about half of the order, I asked if I could take the rest with me for later. She laughed and said, "Well, they won't taste as good later—are you sure you can't finish them now?" The Cheese Curd Lady is proud of her work.

After finishing up at Rocky's, I wandered a couple blocks over to my motel along the river. I sat on the deck with my notebook and curds and watched an absolutely stunning sunset. What a great way to end the day!

Previous page: A Rocky's employee fries up some cheese curds. From top left: Sun setting over the Mississippi River; owner Janet Stearns and her daughter Jaynne Lepke; a fish fry dinner.

![Smoky's Madison]

SMOKY'S Madison

moky's has been Madison's go-to place for steaks for 60 years—especially after a Wisconsin Badgers game. Original owners Leonard and Janet Schmock worked at various bars and restaurants in Madison before buying a supper club called Hogan's on University Avenue, just west of the downtown UW-Madison campus area. The Schmocks picked the name Smoky's to reflect the German pronunciation of their last name, *schmoke*.

Leonard and Janet raised their three children in apartments above the dining room. Throughout their childhoods, the kids held birthday parties in the supper club with their friends. Once they were old enough, they worked in the club clearing tables, washing dishes, and even preparing the food.

Left: The Schmock family— from left, Larry, Tracy, Tim, Bill, Matt, Janet, and Tom.

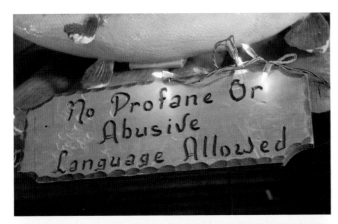

In 1969, Smoky's moved a few doors west to its current location, the former site of Justo's Supper Club. In the four decades since, additions and renovations provided more seating and kitchen space. Today, the Schmocks' sons Tom and Larry run Smoky's, and the club can seat 120 for dinner, plus more at the bar.

During its heyday in the late 1970s, the club often served 300 dinners on a Saturday, and patrons would line up three-deep at the bar. According to Tom, the club's record night came after a Badgers game at nearby Camp Randall Stadium, when nearly 800 dinners were served.

Today, however, business is slower. Tom told of how stiffer drunk driving laws and the early adoption of a Madison-only smoking ban (which later went statewide, of course) has affected the club's draw.

"The business is nothing like it used to be," Tom recalled. "We're selling commodities; it's not a fixed cost. Whenever you get the best, you've got to charge for it, and that prices some people out."

Smoky's menu mostly consists of meat and potatoes, but the club also serves seafood and fish, plus some vegetarian options, including lasagna and stir fries. Once customers are seated, they can dive into a large crock of veggies and a bread basket. Meals include either tomato juice or soup, a salad, and a choice of potato. Many choose the club's signature side, a huge plate of hash browns.

The most popular items at Smoky's are the prime rib, the ribeye, and the open-faced tenderloin sandwich. There's also Janet's special cottage cheese blended with black pepper, caraway seeds, and green onions. Smoky's also offers a fresh-made French roquefort blend dressing for its salads.

Loaded with Wisconsin Badgers memorabilia (including a stuffed badger above the bar), Smoky's is still the place for college football fans to meet up, either before or after the game.

My Take

After finishing my interviews and photos, Tom set up a table for me, and I ordered the filet and hash browns. Smoky's tenderloin filet clocks in at a sizeable 10 ounces, and it was cooked to a perfect medium rare. There was no need for salt, pepper, or any type of condiment for the delicious piece of meat.

To balance the meal, I occasionally nibbled on items from the crock of veggies and then plowed into the two-inch thick order of hash browns that completely covered the plate. Smoky's hash browns are lightly fried, moist, and not greasy. I only wished I'd had room to finish them.

SULLIVAN'S SUPPER CLUB | *Trempealeau*

The building that houses Sullivan's Supper Club has sat alongside the Mississippi River since the turn of the century. Ed Sullivan (no relation to the television great) bought the building in 1968 and made it what it is today, an Irish-themed supper club.

Located a mile north of downtown Trempealeau, just outside the entrance to Perrot State Park, Sullivan's draws hungry diners from La Crosse to Minnesota. Part of the attraction is what Sullivan's calls "a view to dine for." Windows on the west side of the building and the outdoor deck overlook the Mississippi River and the scenic bluffs located on its Minnesota banks. Barges and boats cruise along the river, and an occasional freight train passes between Sullivan's and the shore.

Left: This Packers-themed table is complemented by a Vikings-themed table on the other side of the room.

Owned by Chris Colombo since 2001, Sullivan's can seat 160 and, on a busy night, the club can serve more than 300 dinners. One warm St. Patrick's Day, manager Erik Pyka remembered, the reservation book was already full, but the phone kept ringing with calls from hungry would-be diners. Since the weather was nice, the staff quickly put the outdoor deck to use for cocktails and appetizers.

Sullivan's offers Irish food alongside standard supper club fare. The St. Patrick's Day Taste of Ireland special is a plate heaped with corned beef brisket, cabbage, rutabagas, steamed carrots, and Irish potatoes. Suppers include an extensive all-you-can-eat soup and salad bar and a variety of breads, including the club's own Irish brown bread muffins and choice of potato.

As the Irish say in a common toast to good health, *sláinte!*

TORNADO STEAK HOUSE *Madison*

T he Tornado Steak House is located in the shadow of the state capitol building, tucked away on a side street. It stands alongside a couple of bars and a massage parlor. Owner Henry Doane called the club's location "the last bit of skid row in Madison." The building dates back to the 1850s, and the space above the Tornado used to house the offices of Robert "Fighting Bob" La Follette, a famous son of Wisconsin who, at various times, served as congressman, governor, and senator.

Walking into the Tornado is like taking a trip back in time to the 1950s. In those days, the cocktails were strong, the steaks were huge, and the atmosphere was a combination of dark wood walls and dim lighting. In 1958, the Tornado began its life as a supper club called Crandall's. As a young boy, Henry would dine at

Crandall's with his parents and order the biggest item on the menu, usually a steak. As Henry put it, "I'm a carnivore."

In the 1950s and 1960s, Crandall's was *the* supper club destination in Madison. It closed in 1990 and required some badly needed renovation before Henry opened the Tornado in 1996. Layers of carpeting and glue covered the club's natural wooden floors, and even the sides of the bar. Henry did much of the work himself, including designing the booths for the bar.

"When I look back at how much I spent on just the booths, I probably wouldn't have done that now," recalled Henry.

But the result was more than worthwhile—a perfect time warp back to the 1950s. Henry was

Previous page: Bartender Elliot Hansen serves up a brandy old-fashioned. This page, from top: Tenderloin steak sandwich au jus; shrimp cocktail; bone-in ribeye with hash browns and giant onion ring.

inspired by several Wisconsin supper clubs, including Smoky's in Madison, where he'd visited frequently as a youngster. "I always thought it was a really cool restaurant," Henry recalled.

Henry decided on the name "Tornado" because he wanted a uniquely Midwestern moniker. Tornadoes are a regular aspect of life in and around Madison, of course, and he thought the name projected a sense of energy and power that would get people's attention.

The Tornado's menu features a variety of steaks, including a 20-ounce bone-in tenderloin, a 36-ounce bone-in ribeye, and a 16-ounce New York strip. The club also offers game specialties, including venison, pork, duck, rabbit, and lamb, as well as seafood. Entrées are served with soup or salad, vegetable or potato, and a good-sized loaf of freshly baked bread.

Reservations are recommended, as the Tornado fills up seven nights a week with a mixed crowd

of young professionals, seasoned politicians, and the occasional celebrity. Illustrious patrons include the band Aerosmith and *Happy Days* star Henry Winkler.

Unique to most supper clubs, but de rigueur for the downtown Madison dining scene, is the Tornado's late-night menu, which is served from 10 p.m. to 1 a.m. Long after most supper clubs are closed, the music at the Tornado switches from Sinatra and Nat King Cole to Iggy Pop and the Pixies. The menu also changes to offerings like 8-ounce sirloins, steak or salmon sandwiches, burgers, shimp cocktails, scallops, escargots, soups, salads, and fried cheese curds.

"You can find the idea of 'the supper club,' but to find it with the food you like is really hard to do," Henry said. "I wanted to create the supper club atmosphere and food together. It's about drama— you want to get people's attention. I don't believe in skimping and I know it's a little ridiculous, but it adds to the effect of what a supper club should be."

Northeast Wisconsin
SUPPER CLUBS

STRETCHING FROM THE WESTERN SHORES of Lake Winnebago east to Lake Michigan, the northeastern Wisconsin region is dotted with homes, farmlands, cheese factories, and so many churches that its southernmost part is often referred to as "the Holyland." Starting at the northern end of Lake Winnebago, the Fox River Valley stretches from the paper mills of Appleton all the way north to Green Bay. The far northern area is home to the waterfalls of Marinette County. From there, vineyards lead tourists north to Sturgeon Bay, the gateway to the Door County peninsula. There, cherry orchards, fish boils, and spectacular sunsets abound.

KROPP'S SUPPER CLUB   *Green Bay*

Established in 1946, Kropp's has long been a popular destination for Friday night fish fry in the Green Bay area. Located in Mill Center, which lies several miles northwest of Lambeau Field, Kropp's can be a challenge for newcomers to find. But once you're there, you'll be treated like an old family friend.

Marge Kropp and her daughter Sandra Sheedy currently own Kropp's. Marge waits tables, Sandra is the head chef, and Marge's husband, Merle, serves drinks behind the bar. Marge and Merle have been married for 61 years.

The original building was built in 1904 by Edward O. Lawler, who ran a tavern and inn called Lawler House. Mill Center was full of loggers, and the inn offered overnight rooms upstairs. Lawler House later became the Danceland

Previous page: Merle and Marge Kropp.
Lower left: Mayme Nowack and Marge's sister,
Helen Bergner, are both longtime servers at
Kropp's; members of the kitchen staff.

Ballroom, and in 1946 Isabel and Clarence Kropp bought the business and served fish fry dinners for 35¢ and beers for a nickel. In 1974, Marge took ownership of Kropp's, and in 2005, Sandra and Marge became partners in the business.

To say things have barely changed since 1946 would be an understatement. Waitresses Mayme Nowack and Dorothy Pamperin have been working at Kropp's for over 50 years. Marge's sister Helen Bergner has been there since the 1980s. Sandra has been working behind the scenes since 1978. Kropp's still deals strictly in cash—no credit cards.

Kropp's serves dinner on Wednesdays, Fridays, Saturdays, and on Sundays after Packers games. When asked why the club's not open on Thursdays, Marge simply said that's the way the schedule has always been.

The club has two dining rooms and seats 65, serving 250 dinners on a good night. Chicken and fish are the specialties, but but you can also get steak (except on Fridays). The club gets its fresh, never frozen, fish twice a week from a local supplier.

In the 1960s, Packers players used to frequent Kropp's. "They all used to come in—Bart Starr, Forrest Gregg, Ray Nitschke, but not Coach Lombardi," Merle said.

Customers Glenn and Ann Trustem have been coming to Kropp's since 1958. Glenn said, "Kropp's serves the best battered shrimp, fish, and steaks, and the service is always friendly."

My Take

Before I left, Marge got me a seat in the main dining room for a fish fry. Soon after, I had a plate of fried perch in from of me, along with fore I leave, Marge gets me a seat in the main dining room for a fish fry. Soon after, I have a plate of fried perch in front of me, along with hash browns, rye bread, salad, a cup of clam chowder, and a side order of onion rings. As soon as I tried the perch, I realized why the place is so popular. The large pieces of perch were moist and flavorful, unlike any I'd had before. The hash browns were grilled just right, and the onion rings and soup couldn't have been better.

Later, Marge came by to see how I liked the food. As we chatted, she pointed out her teenage granddaughter, Jennifer, who was helping out in the kitchen. "We hope to keep passing it down in the family," Marge said.

From top: Fried perch; clam chowder; salad.
Right: Grilling hash browns and frying fish in the kitchen.

LOX CLUB · *Combined Locks*

Across from the Appleton Coated paper mill is LOX Club, which began in 1965 under the ownership of Roger "Butter" Vander Wyst and his wife, Betty. The backyard of the club was once the Oakwood Hills Golf Course, which prompted some customers to ask if they needed to be members of the LOX Club to have dinner. Current owners Joe Vander Wyst and his sister, Cindy Brewster, gradually took over the business from their three other siblings after their parents retired in 1990.

Joe has been working at LOX for 34 years. When he was younger, the current lounge area next to the bar served as the family's living room. Bartenders would have to walk through it to get a case of beer or bottles of liquor from the basement. The apartment above the club, which once housed all seven members of the Vander Wyst family, is now an office.

Cindy has worked at LOX since 1970, doing just about everything—washing dishes, clearing tables, waiting tables, and even cooking whenever the kitchen was short staffed. Her daughter Morgan is now the club's hostess.

Most of their employees have been with LOX for as many as 30 years, and so have many of their customers. "I'm serving kiddie cocktails to the grandkids of the people I [once] served kiddie cocktails to," Joe said.

At LOX, customers place their orders at the bar, and they're seated when their tables are ready.

LOX can seat about 90 and serves about 300 on a very busy night. The staff and the customers get to know one another well, Joe said. "Supper clubs are personal places. You get to know families, birthdays, anniversaries."

The menu includes steaks, chicken, and seafood, and specials of beef stroganoff, chicken pot pie, and even chop suey. Tenderloin sandwiches and burgers have always been part of the menu. Supper includes a cheese and cracker selection set out by the bar, as well as soup or salad and rolls. Betty Vander Wyst occasionally makes banana muffins, and during the summer, when she can get garden-fresh zucchini, she'll make zucchini bread.

One of the most special and popular items on the menu is Phoebe's Haddock, which is haddock broiled in garlic seasoning. It was named after Joe and Cindy's aunt, who served as LOX's head chef for 25 years.

THE MILL SUPPER CLUB | Sturgeon Bay

Located outside of Sturgeon Bay, near the intersection of Highways 57 and 42, sits the Mill. You'll find it on your way up to the Door County peninsula. The Mill, built in 1920 by a man named Minor Dagneau, was outfitted with a large windmill on its roof. It was both a tavern that served chicken and fish fry dinners, and a dance hall for entertainment; the second floor was an apartment.

Over the next thirty years, The Mill had a succession of owners, and, at some point, the windmill was taken down. In March 1963, former dairy farmers Milton and Marie Petersilka bought the property. The Petersilkas expanded the club's dining room in 1973.

Below: Owner Don Petersilka, Jr., serves a brandy old-fashioned. Next page: Salad; baked chicken; coleslaw; baked whitefish.

Milton and Marie retired in 1977, selling the Mill to their son Don and his wife Janice. When Don and Janice retired in 1991, the next generation—Don Jr. and his wife Shelly—took over. Generations of Petersilkas continued to live in the upstairs living quarters until 2001.

Steaks at The Mill are hand cut, and two of their most popular cuts are the 6-ounce tenderloin and 8-ounce ribeye. They offer an all-you-can-eat prime rib special on Wednesdays and Saturdays. "Some people have one, others have a few," Don said.

They might start with a 14- or 16-ounce serving, then move on to 10 ounces for additional orders.

113

The Mill also has been serving an all-you-can-eat family-style baked chicken special since the 1950s, plus Lake Michigan whitefish and seafood pasta dishes. Both dining rooms can seat 140, but Don noted that many decide to eat at the bar because it's more social. Customers come from all over, often stopping while on their way up the Door County peninsula.

The Mill is still very much a family operation. Don's mother, Janice, makes the salad dressings. Don and Shelly's kids—Don, Allison, and Anna—help out by tending bar, serving tables for the Friday fish fry, and handling the fish boil—which at the Mill is done indoors on a gas range, rather than outside, like they do farther up in Door County.

PRIME STEER SUPPER CLUB | Kaukauna

You could say that for the Natrop family, supper clubs are in the blood. It all began with the Prime Steer, which Don and Vonnie Natrop opened in 1983. Each of Don's children, Sandy, Dan, and Gary, carried on the family tradition in his or her own way.

Sandy and husband Jerry Rupp own the Wedgewood Supper Club and Golf Course in Omro. Dan Natrop and his wife Laura run Haase's Supper Club in Winnecone. And last but certainly not least, Gary and his wife Lisa took over the Prime Steer from his parents in 1995.

Prime Steer offers weekly specials, pastas, and seafood, but like the name says, the club specializes in steaks—like Gary's three-pound Monster Porterhouse. "It's amazing how many people will come in and eat the whole thing," Gary said.

115

Prime Steer also offers a 34-ounce sirloin for two and a 1-pound Monster Burger. Each meal at Prime Steer includes a choice of potato, and a salad bar featuring pickled gizzards and homemade pasta salads.

Gary began working at the Prime Steer as a boy. He started out as a busboy, and by the age of 16 he had graduated to cooking in the kitchen. Lisa began work there as a bartender in 1987, and Gary wisely ignored the elder Natrops' advice not to date other employees. Today, this next generation of Natrops have three children—Dylan, Madison, and Hunter —who may take over the business one day. The family lives in a house next door to the supper club.

Previous page: From left, Gary, Dylan, Lisa, Hunter, and Madison Natrop; prime rib and baked potato. This page, from top: Porterhouse steak; seafood dinner; prime steer burger; sautéed seafood dinner

Gary races cars at a local track and has a collection of model cars in the bar. The club also features a hunter room decked out with mounted animals that Gary has personally hunted, including an Alaskan moose, a coyote, two wild turkeys, and some deer.

The Prime Steer can seat about 120, and there's ample room for waiting in the bar. When asked how she and Gary attract younger diners to their supper club, Lisa said, "The younger generation is going to chain restaurants, so we keep doing different promos. Once you get them, they come back." The key to the club's success, Lisa said, is its friendly, down-to-earth way of treating customers well.

ROEPKE'S VILLAGE INN — *Chilton*

Above, from left: John, Timothy, Barbara, Jack, and Mike Roepke.

The building that houses Roepke's dates back to 1880, when it was a dance hall, tavern, barbershop and grocery. The original stage of the club's dance hall is still located behind a wall, in a storeroom next to the kitchen.

The supper club sits in the shadow of the St. Charles Catholic Church, which recently closed its doors and was sold to a developer. Roepke's parking lot used to be the site of a cheese factory; nowadays, the club is one of only a handful of buildings on St. Charles Road. The rest of the landscape is mostly farm fields and cows.

John and Rosie Roepke bought Wally's Steak House from owner Joe Dorin in 1968 and renamed it Roepke's Village Inn.

The couple's son, John Jr., began working at Roepke's while attending UW-Madison. His wife Barbara started working at the club in 1975, and the couple married in 1978. In fact, the wedding reception was held in Roepke's banquet room. In 1987, John and Barbara formally took ownership of Roepke's.

The living quarters above the dining room have housed Roepkes since 1968. John and Barbara's son Jack lives there now and tends bar downstairs. In the kitchen, John's brother Mike is the head chef.

The supper club has featured a salad bar since 1968. The bar features several homemade prepared salads, including sweet sauerkraut, and corn, bean, potato, and cucumber salads. You can also find liver pâté, cheese spread, assorted vegetables, and soup. Some Roepke's patrons come just for the soup and salad bar.

Entrées include traditional supper club fare, plus German specialties like wiener schnitzel à la Holstein (topped with two fried eggs), rouladen, and braised pork shank with old world sauerkraut and red wine gravy.

Roepke's can seat 105, plus another 40 in the party room. The club's biggest night is New Year's Eve, when about 650 meals are served. On a busy weekend, Roepke's will serve 400 to 500 dinners.

Barbara noted that people call the supper clubs in the Holyland by their village names; for instance, people call Roepke's "Charlesburg," after

Top left: Kansas City strip steak and baked potato.
Right: Timothy Roepke serves a grasshopper.

My Take

One of the highlights of my visit to Roepke's was trying the club's best dishes with John and Barbara. We enjoyed great conversation while trying four excellent meals—Kansas City strip, wiener schnitzel à la Holstein, pork shank, and salmon. I also enjoyed a sampling of the salad bar and the club's delicious French onion soup. After dinner, Barbara brought over a wonderful slice of white chocolate raspberry swirl cheesecake for me to try. Before I left, John invited me to have a grasshopper at the bar. It was a fun and friendly evening, and I returned to my motel relaxed, full, and happy.

the unincorporated community in which Roepke's is located. Holyland supper clubs have one advantage over those in more urban locations: their only competition is other supper clubs. There are no chain restaurants for many miles.

When asked what makes Roepke's successful, John said, "We've always had quality food, we cut our own meat, we mix a good drink, and [we] offer a good price." Barbara added, "You do your thing the best you can and not worry about other places out there. You've got to love people in this business."

Right: wiener schnitzel à la Holstein; cheesecake slice.

SCHWARZ'S SUPPER CLUB — *New Holstein*

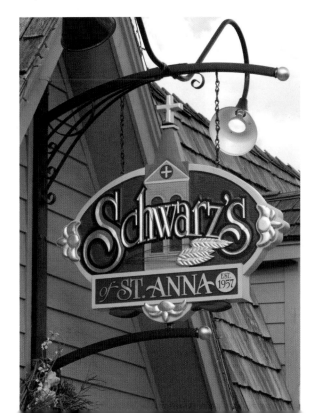

While many supper clubs are destinations, Schwarz's gives the word new meaning. It would be next to impossible for someone to accidentally drive by the club on the way to somewhere else. Schwarz's mailing address is New Holstein, but the club is located in the hamlet of St. Anna (pronounced "Saint Ann" by the local residents) and surrounded by farm fields.

Like most other supper clubs in the Holyland, Schwarz's sits in the shadow of a nearby church, St. Ann's. An image of the church steeple is incorporated into the club's logo by the front door.

121

Below: Customers review the menu; owners Lisa and John Schwarz. Next page: Ribeye steak with a twice-baked potato; relish tray; fried calamari; red velvet cake.

Schwarz's was opened in 1957 by the parents of current owner John Schwarz. John took over the business in 1971, after his father passed away. He's still running the club today, with his wife Lisa, son Charley, and daughter-in-law Stephanie.

"We use 23,000 pounds of prime rib during a year, which works out to about a thousand pounds per month," John said. Schwarz's cuts of prime rib range from an 8- to 10-ounce petite to a 48- to 52-ounce prime rib for two.

"We have about 20 to 25 people who polish off their 50-ounce cut of prime rib, their salad, and their potatoes, and they come out to the bar and have a grasshopper. They're still hungry," John marveled.

Reservations are not accepted. Customers sit down at the bar for a drink, and the waitstaff come by to take their orders. When tables are ready with their salads, relish tray, and bread, their names are called and they're seated. On a busy night, Schwarz's may serve as many as 700 people. With a dining room that fits a maximum of 140 to 150, the wait can be up to two hours, Lisa said.

Customers come from all over, including one couple who makes the six-hour round trip from Barrington, Illinois. For those who don't want to make such a long drive home, Schwarz's operates a bed and breakfast next door.

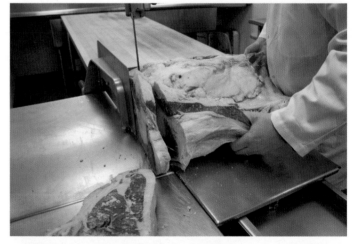

Right: Charley Schwarz displays his prime rib cuts with his wife, Stephanie.
Next page: The Red Magic broiler in action.

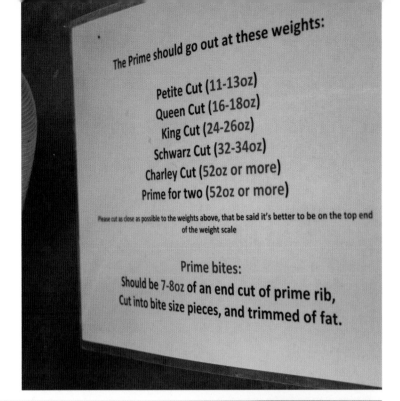

The Prime should go out at these weights:

Petite Cut (11-13oz)
Queen Cut (16-18oz)
King Cut (24-26oz)
Schwarz Cut (32-34oz)
Charley Cut (52oz or more)
Prime for two (52oz or more)

Please cut as close as possible to the weights above, that be said it's better to be on the top end of the weight scale

Prime bites:
Should be 7-8oz of an end cut of prime rib,
Cut into bite size pieces, and trimmed of fat.

My Take

Charley Schwarz showed me how he uses a band saw to make the initial cuts in a side of beef, something I'd never seen before. Once the major cuts are made, he cuts the individual steaks by hand. Charley mentioned that he's noticed that the weight of the sides of beef has been going down, as farmers have begun to send their cattle to market a bit earlier.

The steaks at Schwarz's are cooked in a Red Magic vertical broiler that dates from the 1950s. It's similar to the Astro Ray used at The Silvercryst. The steaks cook faster and retain more flavor in these types of broilers, since both sides are cooked at the same time.

After finishing up for the evening, John and Lisa invited me to have a drink at the bar and order some supper. Having seen all those fabulous cuts of meat, I briefly considered ordering the 52-ounce Charley Cut of prime rib. Wisely, I opted instead for a well-marbled ribeye, cooked medium rare and served with a double-baked potato. I topped this great meal off with a luscious slice of red velvet cake.

SHAFFER PARK RESORT AND SUPPER CLUB — *Crivitz*

Shaffer Park Resort is located on the Peshtigo River on the western edge of Crivitz. The resort features 2 motels with a total of 27 rooms, a 3-bedroom cottage, a tennis court, and a heated pool. In the center of it all sits a large supper club that owes its existence to some tasty fried chicken.

The story starts with Ursula "Grandma" Shaffer. Ursula, a Yugoslavian immigrant, married John Shaffer and lived on a farm just across the Peshtigo River from the current site of Shaffer Park Resort. On the farm, Grandma Shaffer used to supplement her income by making fried chicken for the threshers who came in to work the area farms. She became known for the quality of her fried chicken, and its popularity gave her the idea to open a restaurant.

Previous page: Owners Mark and Amy Shaffer. Left: Postcard featuring an aerial photo by Mark. Shaffer Park Resort is in the foreground and his grandmother's farm is across the Peshtigo River.

She persuaded her son John Jr. to purchase property on the Peshtigo River in 1946, and in 1947, he opened a one-room beer bar with a stone fireplace. The bar is still part of the main supper club's building today.

In those days, Grandma ran the kitchen with her sister Stella, Stella's husband Goldie, and their son Bob. The fried chicken business boomed during the 1950s. John Jr. and his wife June also worked at the restaurant, and they took over the business after Grandma passed away. John's son, current owner Mark Shaffer, began working at the supper club at age 15. At that same tender age, his grandma taught him how to cook her famous fried chicken.

Mark took over the supper club in 1990, but John Jr. held on to the motels for seven more years. Eventually, Mark took over the motels when his dad retired to a nearby farm. He lived there until the summer of 2012, when he passed away at the age of 92.

127

Top: Fried chicken with
french fries and cole slaw.
Right: Perch dinner with
baked potato and cole slaw.

Grandma's fried chicken is based on a European recipe, and it's a tightly held family secret, Mark said. The not-so-secret part is that the chicken is coated in an egg mixture, lightly breaded, and fried in fresh lard. Every day, the kitchen uses a fresh batch of lard.

The fried chicken is cooked to order; the time from preparation to plate is 30 minutes. Customers place their orders at the bar, and when their tables are ready, they're seated and given a relish tray and rolls.

Shaffer's supper club menu is simple: fried chicken and fried fish, with no steaks. Mark said that his grandma warned him about ever serving steaks at the restaurant. Her philosophy was simple: Stick with your specialty. The specialty is so closely associated with Shaffer Park that people in this part of Wisconsin often refer to Crivitz as "the chicken place."

Mark explained that the club began cooking four-and-a-half-pound birds—a full pound bigger than they had in the past—because the weight keeps the meat moist during frying. The chicken is also cooked in open fryers, rather than pressure cookers. Mark said, "By serving the food our way, it's always consistent."

Supper choices at Shaffer's include chicken dinners, chicken livers or gizzards, Canadian perch or walleye, shrimp or scallops, and chopped sirloin. All entrees include dinner rolls, assorted relish tray, whole cranberry sauce, baked potato or french fries, coleslaw or tossed salad, and homemade cookies, including a sugar cookie.

Shaffer's also makes its own unique coleslaw, which is so popular that some diners ask for a second portion of slaw instead of the potato.

In the past few years, Shaffer Park Resort has been closing just after deer season and reopening in April. Mark says business during the winter hasn't been as good as it used to be—especially at the height of the snowmobile era, in the '60s and '70s. However, during the summer and fall, the resort's motel rooms are full, and the supper club cooks a lot of chicken dinners.

My Take

After I finished my interview with Mark and his wife, Amy, she placed an order of chicken, walleye, and perch for us to share.

First up was an order of chicken gizzards. The gizzards were served hot, with a light gravy. Upon first bite, I realized they were an acquired taste, but other customers certainly enjoy them. One customer in particular, Amy said, always orders a plate of gizzards and french fries for dinner.

The fried chicken, on the other hand, was wonderful. The light breading was seasoned just right, and the meat on all the pieces was plump and juicy. All the pieces—even the wings—were bigger than any piece of chicken I've had before.

The walleye was wonderful and fresh, fried in vegetable oil, not lard. The fried perch was meaty, moist, and tasty.

Shaffer's coleslaw was the best, simplest slaw I've ever had, with large slices of cabbage. I, too, would have traded a potato for a second portion of slaw.

As we had our supper, the conversation got a bit more personal, as I told the Shaffers about my own Grandma Shafer (spelled with one "f"), who cooked much-loved Italian meals, as well as my high school experience cooking chicken at KFC. I learned that both Mark and Amy are seasoned pilots. Mark owns a four-seat Cessna 172 that the couple flies to Door County or Green Bay for supper. In fact, Mark was the photographer who shot the bird's-eye view of the resort shown on the club's postcard.

After dinner, Mark made some of his specialty drinks at the bar, including a special blend of liquors topped with a bit of Bacardi 151 (rum with a 75.5% alcohol content). The drink is then lit on fire and sprinkled with cinnamon, creating a sparking shot that lights up like the Fourth of July

It was truly a memorable evening. Mark and Amy may have been just acquaintances of mine, but they certainly treated me like a lifelong friend.

SUNSET SUPPER CLUB *Fond du Lac*

Sunset Supper Club is located about 50 feet from the eastern shore of Lake Winnebago. The site was once home to a coach stop and general store, built in 1854 by Valentine and Margaret Mengel. Back in 1906, the Mengels' son Peter turned the place into a grocery, tavern, and soda fountain. After Peter's death in 1942, the business became the Club Sunset Supper Club. Later, it became the Sunset Shores, and finally the Sunset Supper Club.

Current owners Scott and Kelly Huck worked at the Sunset for eight years before purchasing the club in 1992. For nine years they lived above the club, and today they rent the apartment to the club's head chef.

During the couple's twenty years of ownership, they've kept the traditional supper club staples on the menu but added more casual items, including pastas, burgers, and sandwiches. They've also added some specialty items, such as the delicious prime rib fritters, which consists of pieces of prime rib that are breaded and pressure fried.

The Sunset's main room seats 120 people, and the club serves about 300 dinners a night on weekends. As the club's name suggests, the bar and dining room boast spectacular views of the sunset over the lake.

In addition to the Sunset's regular customers, diners come from all over the Midwest for the terrific year-round recreation on Lake Winnebago, and the annual Experimental Aircraft Association (EAA) event in Oshkosh.

From top: Old menus in a frame on the wall; members of the waitstaff. Next page: Prime rib and BBQ rib meals; the dock on Lake Winnebago; owner Scott Huck serves a brandy old-fashioned.

North Central Wisconsin
SUPPER CLUBS

THE NORTH CENTRAL REGION OF WISCONSIN is home to Wisconsin's Northwoods, where year-round recreation and logging share space with the Chequamegon-Nicolet National Forest, Indian reservations, casinos, and, according to some, the Hodag, a mythical horned creature said to live in Rhinelander. Bordered on its north side by Michigan's Upper Peninsula, this region was once full of hideouts frequented by Depression-era Chicago mobsters and criminals on the run. These legendary criminals include John Dillinger, who escaped during a shootout with federal agents at the Little Bohemia Lodge, which is still open today.

ANTLERS SUPPER CLUB *Bonduel*

ocated in the center of downtown Bonduel, the Antlers Supper Club offers a decor that could be either intimidating or interesting, depending on your personal views on hunting and taxidermy. The main attractions are: about a dozen deer and rams, a huge black bear, and approximately 200 deer antlers around the bar.

This turn-of-the-century building has been home to Antlers since 2000, when William and Sandy Springstroh bought the business. Prior to the Springstrohs' purchase, the club was known for four years as the Bookwoods Supper Club, and for two decades before that it was the Royal Inn Supper Club. In its very early days, the club included a dance hall on the main floor and a boxing ring upstairs. Current owners Lance and Vicki Olson bought Antlers Supper Club from the Springstrohs, who are Vicki's parents, in 2008 (Lance's father, Jerry, now lives above the club).

The club's name, and the antlers that are proudly mounted inside it, came from a deer farm owned by Vicki's father. As deer age, they grow more aggressive, so the farm would cut their antlers off so they couldn't injure each other. The antlers found a home at the supper club. One of the deer heads on the wall belonged to a breeder buck at the farm; some of the others were its offspring. There's also one mounted deer in the bar who sings; its main purpose is to surprise unsuspecting customers.

In the dining room stands a 500-pound black bear. Lance shot it during a hunting trip in Manitoba, Canada, in 1999. A bee is perched on its nose, and surrounding it are real fawns from the deer farm who died young or were stillborn. Lance purchased the Rocky Mountain rams from a collector.

Clockwise from top left: Seafood Alfredo with garlic bread; pan-fried walleye and American fries; 14-ounce tenderloin with broasted potatoes; ribeye steak with cheese-and-onion hash browns. Next page: Lance and Vicki Olson with their children, Remington and Alex Brandt, in the foreground.

While the antlers and game attract plenty of curiosity-seekers to Antlers, the main attraction is the food. Traditional supper club fare and some pasta dishes make up the bulk of the menu. German specials are served on Thursdays; these include a variety of schnitzels, rouladen, and schweinshaxen (pork shanks). On Sunday, the club offers a variety of omelets alongside the full menu, from 9 a.m. until closing.

Many customers are local, while others come from as far as 30 to 40 miles away. The dining room seats 80 to 85, and the club can serve about 200 dinners on a busy night. Lance said that Antlers is known for steaks in large portion sizes, from 22 to 24 ounces—enough to satisfy a hearty appetite or to share with a hungry bear.

BERNARD'S COUNTRY INN · *Stevens Point*

Trained European chef Bernard Kurzawa prepares veal, duck, and German specialties at this Stevens Point supper club bearing his name. Born in Berlin, Germany, Bernard has worked in kitchens all over the world, eventually landing at Chicago's exclusive Mid-America Club. While there, he met his wife, Irene. Her parents owned a summer cottage in the Mosinee area, and when the opportunity arose to open a restaurant on the north side of Stevens Point in 1973, Bernard's Country Inn was born.

Business was slow until a prominent executive from nearby Sentry Insurance came in one night to check the club out. He loved the food and spread the word around town. Soon, Bernard's was a favorite destination in Stevens Point. These days, business is a bit slower, but on occasion it fills to capacity. Irene reported that the club recently served a record-setting Easter Sunday brunch.

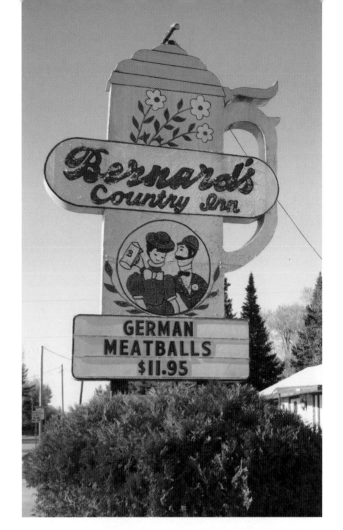

Previous page: Bernard and Irene Kurzawa in their souvenir shop. This page, from top: Jaeger schnitzel in a brown wine sauce with mushrooms, onions, and spatzle; wiener schnitzel served with lemon and spaetzle; sauerbraten in a sweet and sour brown sauce with red cabbage and a potato dumpling.

141

"Serving fine cuisine food is not a money maker in this country; selling 100 pizzas per day in 20 stores is where the money is," Bernard said. "For me, it's expensive and difficult to train new chefs."

The menu at Bernard's features many German dishes, including wiener schnitzel, jaeger schnitzel, zigeuner schnitzel, sauerbraten, some duck and chicken dishes, plus steaks and seafood. The main dining room holds about 60 people, and the spacious bar area includes a small gift shop with souvenirs and magazines that feature Bernard on the cover.

In short, Bernard's is all about good food, seasoned by Chef Bernard's many years of experience.

My Take

Chef Bernard is known to restaurant industry veterans around Stevens Point as a somewhat gruff character who doesn't mince words. He lived up to that reputation early on in my visit. One question in particular—whether Bernard's had any specialty items on the menu—provoked a salty rebuke not fit for these pages. Bernard indignantly declared that he doesn't make specialty dishes because "all my dishes are great!" As we sat at the bar and talked, Bernard warmed up, and we bonded over experiences we'd both had in Berlin. We discussed German food, beer and wine, and the changes Berlin has gone through over the last few decades.

Just before I left, Bernard brought out a book published in 1914 entitled *Kochkunst-Führer* (possibly a German reprint of *Le Guide Culinaire*, which was originally released in 1903). The book, which was perhaps the finest cookbook by the famous chef Auguste Escoffier, had been a gift from a customer. Escoffier was a French-born chef who forged his reputation with haute cuisine. Escoffier revolutionized and modernized the restaurant menu, the art of cooking, and the organization of the professional kitchen. Chefs still use his methods in their kitchens to this day. Bernard treasures the book for two reasons—first, it's autographed by Escoffier himself; and second, Bernard used the book while he was training at the side of one of Escoffier's students in Berlin.

When it was time for me to go, Bernard, who previously had been quite blustery with his opinions, said quietly, "See you."

BUCK-A-NEER SUPPER CLUB | Stratford

The building that is now home to the Buck-A-Neer began life in the late 1800s as a blacksmith's shop before being converted into a roadhouse. Later, World War I veterans purchased the business and turned it into a wayside with gas pumps and a tavern. They named it Paris Avenue and gave it the look of a French country house. The doors and windows were imported from France; the small back bar, still in use today, came from Germany.

In 1958, a stone facade was added with red granite and quartz from local farm fields. Owner Frank Obenberger turned it into a restaurant called "Buck-aneer," after the deer and other game hunting that occurred in the area. While the building's original neon sign still reads "Buck-aneer," these days the name has taken on a pirate-inspired theme, and it's known as the Buck-A-Neer.

Left: Rich Seubert's football memorabilia. Below: Jean, Roy, Tom, and Ann Seubert at the bar.

The Seubert family's ownership of the club began when Dick and Celine purchased the club in 1973. They lived above the club with their sons, Tom and Roy. Roy and his wife, Jean, took ownership in 1998, and Roy, Tom, and their wives still live in the two apartments above the Buck-A-Neer.

Most taverns and supper clubs in Wisconsin have at least a few Green Bay Packers items on the walls. At the Buck-A-Neer, Packers souvenirs are outnumbered by New York Giants memorabilia in honor of Tom's son Rich Seubert, who spent eight seasons as an offensive guard for the Giants. At the entrance to the town, just around the corner from the Buck-A-Neer, an official sign lists the younger Seubert's achievements.

Tom Seubert has served as the chef at the Buck-A-Neer since the late '70s. People come from all over for his all-you-can-eat steak, his tenderloin kabobs and shrimp, and his Friday fish fry specials, which include an all-you-can-eat salad bar. Business has been good—Tom recalls serving 2,000 dinners one weekend—but the next generation of Seuberts have no interest in taking over the business. Tom hopes when the family decides to retire, a new buyer will keep the current Buck-A-Neer going.

My Take

Tom made sure I got a plate of tenderloin kabobs and shrimp, plus a heaping order of fried cheese curds, before I left. As the club started filling up with customers, Tom told me that the Buck-A-Neer was one of the first establishments to serve homemade fried cheese curds, although a few other supper clubs around the state also make that claim (including Rocky's in Stoddard). As it was, I found both the fried cheese curds and the steak and shrimp dish to be absolutely wonderful—no wonder the club was so crowded!

MAIDEN LAKE SUPPER CLUB — *Mountain*

Maiden Lake Supper Club is nestled along Maiden Lake in the southern half of the 800,000-acre Chequamegon-Nicolet National Forest. Its cocktail decks overlooking the lake, which were modeled after those at Ishnala in Lake Delton, are the club's "claim to fame," said owner Michael Jon (MJ) Dinkelman. "I have to say that we're the best supper club within 60 miles in any direction," MJ added.

At Maiden Lake, orders are taken at the bar. When their tables are ready, diners sit down to a relish tray and cheese and crackers. The club's gorgonzola-topped tenderloin is popular, but MJ said the club is best known for its walleye. "We go through 5,500 pounds in a year," he said.

The building has long been known as the Maiden Lake Resort, and its history goes back about 100 years. According to MJ, it was owned by Bunny Erickson in the 1950s, LeRoy White from 1958 to 1968, and Ed and Loretta Zebrasky from 1968 to 1978. Next to the supper club, the Zebraskys built cabins, which tourists would rent for the summer.

Before buying the club, MJ's parents, Mike and Georgia Dinkelman, lived in South Milwaukee. Mike was a captain at the South Milwaukee Fire Department, and the couple had a cabin just north of Maiden Lake. They would often dine together at the supper club. When the club was put up for sale in 1978, Mike decided to take a risk and buy it, which meant giving up his position and pension at the fire department. In 1985, the couple started selling off the adjacent cabins to finance such improvements to the club as the three-level wooden deck and the landscaping that extends to the lakeshore. The cabins are now condos, some of which are available for rent by their respective owners.

Above: Mike Dinkelman's
collection of model firefighter
equipment and mementos.
Below: Perch fry; Mike, Georgia,
Trina, and MJ Dinkelman.

MJ and his wife Trina, who had lived in Milwaukee, moved to Lakewood after Trina became pregnant. They bought the supper club from Mike and Georgia in 2003 and moved into the house next door. These days, their two teenage children, Zachary and Lindsey, help out around the club.

The menu offers steaks, seafood, chicken, and shrimp de Jonghe, which is not commonly seen on supper club menus this far north. The club also offers unique specials, such as lamb tenderloin and blood orange scallops.

"It's a supper club atmosphere, but we don't have competition for high quality," MJ said. "We're priced $10 more per head. I'm pricey for the area,

and I know that, but we have a lot of Chicago people who laugh at the prices because they're so low compared to Chicago. I'll do 70 percent of my gross in 4 months."

Friday nights are the club's busiest, with wait times of up to two hours. The club doesn't take reservations, but MJ said guests plan accordingly. "If you want to eat at eight, you get here at six," he said.

One secret of the club's success is its consistency, MJ added. "With four family members here, we make sure everything is done right: portion sizes, drinks and food," he said. "That's why people keep coming back."

MAMA'S SUPPER CLUB *Minocqua*

Above: Paintings of Irene, Angela ("Mama"), and Thomas Chiolino.

The story of Mama's Supper Club begins with Angela Gentile, who traveled from Sicily to the United States once to visit her brother and decided to stay. She met James Chiolino, and together, they raised a family in Ironwood, Michigan. Around the age when most people retire, Angela and James purchased a run-down, shuttered bar outside of Minocqua on Curtis Lake that had been named the Illinois Tavern. The place had been quite famous in its day for its 49-cent chicken dinners.

The little tavern on Highway 70 had been closed for some time, and the building was in terrible shape. But the couple renovated the building and reopened it as the Bella Vista, which served pizza to a small but loyal crowd. One steady customer, Doc Mellis, called Angela "Mama." The name stuck, and it soon became a part of the business. The restaurant first changed its name to Mama's Bella Vista, and then became simply Mama's.

The family expanded the building, and in the early '60s, the Chiolinos' son Thomas and daughter Irene Clothier came in to help with the growing business. Today, Thomas's wife Judy, her son Tony, and his wife Cheryl continue the tradition of Mama's. The family still lives in the two homes next to Mama's, and various children and grandchildren help out when they're not in school. As Judy put it, "It's all about family."

Mama's can seat 100. Back when the kitchen stayed open until late, the restaurant could serve 500 dinners a night. These days, its capacity on a busy summer Friday is about 350.

The club serves American and Italian fare, steaks, seafood, pastas, and pizza, and diners can enjoy the view of Curtis Lake as they eat. The pizza dough and pastas are made from scratch using Angela's original recipes from Sicily. Judy said, "They are truly 'a kettle of this,' 'a bucket of this,' [and] 'a handful of flour.' It takes some effort to get the right amount."

Once, Judy recalled, Angela was using some olive oil to stretch out pizza dough, and the slippery oil caused her to lose her wedding ring. They were about to ask all the customers who'd

*Above: Cheryl, Tony,
and Judy Chiolino.*

ordered pizza to check their pies for a ring. Fortunately, it was found lying under a table in the kitchen. There's also the story of a customer who would take Mama's all-you-can-eat spaghetti special to the extreme, eating about 2 pounds of mostaccioli every time he'd come in for dinner.

Some members of the staff have been there for two or three decades. "It's a family atmosphere; everyone is treated like family," Cheryl said. "When they reach the 20-year mark, we give them a watch. The joke is that someone has to retire or die for a job opening to become available."

Angela spent her later years chatting with customers—especially those who spoke Italian. After she passed away in 1975, Irene became "Mama." Later, Judy became "Mama Judy," and now the "Mama" designation has passed on to Cheryl, who said, "People always come in and ask if I'm Mama."

"It's a very satisfying business," Judy said. In particular, Judy enjoys "getting to know customers, and they bring in their children, who then bring in their children." The Mama's tradition shows no sign of ending.

MARTY'S PLACE NORTH   *Arbor Vitae*

Marty's Place North began as a farmhouse in the 1920s, later morphed into a resort with cabins, and finally became a supper club when Marty Cady and his wife, Judy, bought the run-down building in 1982. The couple already owned a club named Marty's in Kimberly, a town about 175 miles south of Arbor Vitae, so the new club was dubbed Marty's Place North.

Marty and Judy updated the club with warm lighting and created a cozy atmosphere, including restoring the resort's original fireplace. A birch bark canoe made by local legend Ferdy Goode hangs over the bar area. The canoe is taken down once a year and soaked in nearby Little Spider Lake to keep it in shape.

The red signs emblazoned with the Cady family coat of arms were taken from the exterior of Marty's Kimberly location, which was sold in 1984. The signs surround the most requested table at the club, the round-room gazebo. This eight-seat table feels like a private room, yet is the center of attention. The table is illuminated by a large operating room-style light with brass gilding.

Left: A birchbark canoe hangs above the bar.
Below: Andrew Teece and Andrea Cady-Teece.

Marty and Judy's daughter, Andrea Cady-Teece, worked at Marty's as a girl. Today, Andrea and her husband, Andrew, are in the process of buying the supper club from Judy (Marty has since passed away). Their children, Dayton and Delaney, work with their parents; perhaps one day they will take over the club.

While Andrea and Andrew continue to offer classic supper club menu items, they also work with head chef Tim Wydeven to create new dishes based on their customers' comments and requests. This club's focus is on quality over quantity, Andrea said.

The club now offers several new weekly specials. On Monday nights, Marty's serves German specials of rouladen, wiener schnitzel, and spaetzle. Thursday is pasta night. The crowd favorites, however, are the Friday fish fry and Saturday duck dinners. In fact, the duck dinners are so popular that customers call ahead and reserve their ducks to make sure the club won't run out.

The new menu focuses on hand-cut steaks and hand-breaded seafood dishes, plus homemade desserts like crème brûlée and strawberry schaum torte. Craft beers and an expanded selection of wines are offered in response to customers' requests.

The banquet room downstairs is said to be home to the club's resident ghost, George. Andrea said that George has been seen by several different people, each of whom give similar descriptions of him. She believes that George had been the original owner of the farmhouse. George is said to be pretty harmless, as his primary preoccupation is making lights go out three at a time, mostly when Judy isn't around. Now that Judy is selling the business, Andrea wondered if he'll act up a bit more.

Above: Light fixture with brass gilding.
Right: The popular round-room gazebo table.

Around the time Marty's Place North first opened in 1982, Marty Cady wrote this poem:

Women who cook and do the dishes
should be granted these three wishes
a grateful mate
a well kissed cheek
and dinner at Marty's once a week

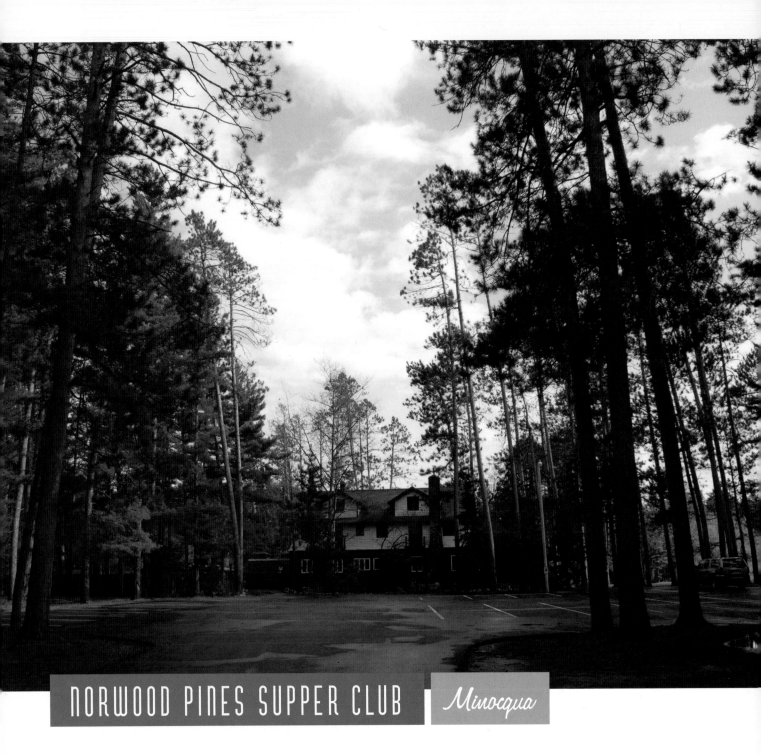

NORWOOD PINES SUPPER CLUB | *Minocqua*

The history of Norwood Pines would make a great Hollywood thriller—full of drama, mystery, and intrigue. In 1937, businessman Frank Tillman purchased 200 acres outside of Minocqua and built a resort called Norwood Pines that featured a hotel, restaurant, and cabins overlooking Patricia Lake. Some of the available activities included skeet shooting and horseback riding.

Four years later, as he and his wife Monica were going through a bitter divorce, Frank sold the resort for $25,000. However, before the new owners had moved in, Monica allegedly stole thousands of dollars worth of items from the resort and put a curse on the business.

Some years later, Frank arrived back in town with a briefcase full of money and paid $10,000 for the missing items, as well as settled other overdue debts.

Even though the debts had been paid off, Monica's "curse" seemed to have an effect. Over the next several decades, Norwood Pines changed hands fifteen times, and none of the owners seemed to be successful. Some of the owners fell victim to bizarre accidents and met unpleasant ends: one fell out of a tree, for example, while another was run over by a train.

When the current owners—the Teichmiller brothers—looked into buying the long-closed Norwood Pines in 1995, the local bank let them know that the place was said to be haunted. One banker told of personally witnessing upstairs windows opening and closing on their own on several occasions. John Teichmiller has heard voices, and Tom Teichmiller said that he's found furniture that has been rearranged overnight. In any case, the brothers got a good deal from the bank to buy the place.

The brothers also own T. Murtaugh's Pub and Eatery and Belle Isle Sports Bar and Grille in Minocqua. When they bought Norwood Pines, John recalled, "The building was in phenomenal shape; however, the tables and plates and silverware had been pilfered, nothing matched, and the reputation of the business was gone." At that point,

Above: Owners Tom and John Teichmiller stand by the dining room fireplace.

161

Above: The Norwood Pines version of a relish tray, called "complimentary appetizers."
Below: Steak with sautéed mushrooms and red-wine-and-peppercorn sauce.

all but 25 acres of the original 200-acre estate had been sold. Tom moved into the upstairs hotel rooms and stayed there for about three years. Today, the rooms are unused.

Initially, three Teichmiller brothers were partners in the club, but Tom and John later bought out their brother Andy's share. After the brothers made it to their 13th year of ownership, they figured the curse had been broken—no previous owner had stuck around for longer than 12 years. Thirteen was their lucky number!

"The last three years have been great," Tom said, explaining that they host numerous events for local groups and clubs. John added, "People wanted this place to be successful. They've now become repeat customers."

The menu features several dishes prepared Oscar style (topped with steamed asparagus, crab meat, and hollandaise sauce), including veal, chicken, shrimp, and tenderloin. Other offerings are an all-you-can-eat fish fry, steaks, seafood, and pasta. The club's most popular dish, however, is its filet stuffed with sautéed portobello mushrooms and garlic, topped with melted burgundy butter.

Meals at the Norwood Pines begin with a variation on the supper club relish tray. Called "complimentary appetizers," the Norwood Pines version consists of homemade tortilla chips, cranberry salsa, fruit, and the club's pasta salad of the day.

On a busy summer night, the club can serve 400 or more customers; during the off season, that number drops to about 250. The dining room and bar have wood-burning fireplaces, and most tables overlook Patricia Lake and the pine trees of the adjacent woods. Observant guests might spot an occasional whitetail deer roaming the grounds just outside the supper club.

PINEWOOD SUPPER CLUB *Mosinee*

Tucked away on a scenic corner of Half Moon Lake, the Pinewood Supper Club began as the Pine Top Bar and Bath House in 1898. It sat the end of a logging trail, where the logs would be sent down the Mosinee Flowage, another large lake, toward the Wisconsin River.

In the 1930s, a bigger bar and dance hall were added to the small bar and bath house, and it became the Pine Top Lodge. In 1940, the Linder family purchased the Pine Top and began serving food. In 1960, Al and Jenny Conner bought the club and renamed it the Pinewood Supper Club.

THE
PINEWOOD
SUPPER CLUB

MOSINEE, WISCONSIN

YOUR HOSTS
The Allens

In 1974, Al and Sally Allen bought the club. Al had been the general manager of the Hot Fish Shop in Stevens Point for many years. Eight years later, Al and Sally's son Steve bought the club with his wife Joan, who had already been working at the Pinewood for a couple of years.

These days, Steve runs the kitchen and Joan works the front of house as hostess. The couple lives next door in a house that was built in 1982, and they both say that no matter what the season, the view of Half Moon Lake from the club and their home is always spectacular. The bluff over-looking the lake has been used for outdoor wedding ceremonies, and in the summer they added a dock for boats.

The Pinewood features steaks and prime rib, but Steve also serves fresh several fish and seafood specials. His cracker-crusted, pan-fried walleye and crab-stuffed salmon are popular dishes, as are the batter-fried shrimp, crab puffs, and haddock fish fry. One steak special is named after the couple's son: Steak Garrison is a tenderloin filet stuffed with bacon from Nueske's, a legendary Wisconsin meat purveyor, and topped with melted cheese.

Above left: Owners Steve and Joan Allen. Left: Customers Carol McCort Brennan and Mike Brennan toast to the start of a good meal.

Next page: Steak Garrison; relish tray; gator balls; crab puffs.

One menu item that will make you think twice is the "gator balls," which are three fried balls made of ground alligator tail meat and a few other ingredients, served with a special dipping sauce. When asked about the dish's risqué name, Steve laughed and said, "Of course we call it that—that's why we sell so much of it."

The club's relish tray features an array of fresh vegetables, which are purchased at the local farmer's market when they're in season. The staff cuts the fresh veggies each evening, and the carrot skins and broccoli ends aren't just thrown away. No, at the Pinewood, they're fed to a group of fainting goats.

The goats are just one part of Steve and Joan's environmental awareness policy, which includes recycled paper take-out boxes instead of plastic clamshells, environmentally friendly soaps and paper napkins, and a fuel-efficient car that doubles as a mobile advertisement for the Pinewood.

The Pinewood seats 140 and can serve as many as 300 dinners on weekend nights. A large banquet room on the other side of the building is used for weddings and private functions.

Steve and Joan's two children, Garrison and Jacquelyn, have been working at the Pinewood "since they were old enough," and will likely be the next to take over the family business.

THE SILVERCRYST — *Wautoma*

Above: Bartender Susan Corning serves up a brandy old-fashioned from the uniquely decorated bar.

The Silvercryst sits on the eastern shore of the 700-acre Silver Lake, a popular recreational lake on Highway 21 in Wautoma. Its history begins in 1894, when a fishing cottage was built on the site to welcome visitors arriving in the area via a new railroad line. The cottage slowly grew into a small resort that offered lodging, food, and drinks, with a little gambling on the side. According to one story, during Prohibition the local sheriff would often be tipped off about an upcoming raid by federal agents, and he'd arrive to help the resort's proprietors hide the gaming machines and alcohol in another location.

In 1952, Jerry Honl and his father, Barney, bought the business and turned it into a supper club. Jerry sold the Silvercryst to the club's head cook, Dick Pfaller, in 1992. Dick retired in 2000 and sold the club to his brother Mike Pfaller

(who also worked in the club's kitchen) and the club's bartender, James Heck. Mike and James had both been working at the Silvercryst for more than a decade, so the transition was seamless.

The wooden design of the bar dates back to the mid-1970s, and the kitchen was built around three 1950s Astro-Ray broilers. They're the key to the popularity of the Silvercryst's steaks. According to Mike, the Astro-Rays cook steaks better and faster than anything else available today. Since they're no longer made, Mike keeps some spare parts around for repairs.

The menu at the Silvercryst includes lots of seafood and a thin-crust pizza made from a recipe that's been around since 1955. It also features a one-pound pork chop, one-pound tenderloin, South

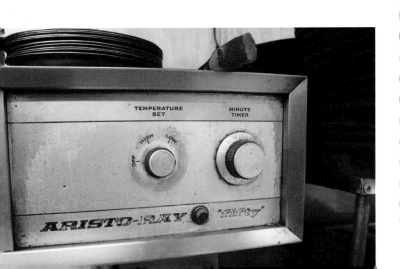

The SILVERCRYST

WAUTOMA, WISC.

• Zesty Cocktails
• Wonderful Food

Featuring
ARISTO-RAY STEAKS
BROASTED CHICKEN

African lobsters, and a set of original salad dressing interpretations called Silvercryst Selects, which are so popular that they're bottled and sold in area grocery stores. On Fridays, the club features an all-you-can-eat breaded and fried haddock or baked cod, and fried chicken. "You can mix and match the fish and chicken," James said. Perch is also served, but it's a single portion, not all-you-can-eat.

The club's two dining rooms seat around 165 people, and the lounge and entertainment area, where live music is performed on Saturdays, can seat another 80. Out front sits a large statue of a bull named Boris, who has greeted Silvercryst customers since 1965. (A smaller version of the bull, named Bingo, is used in parades.)

The Silvercryst also still offers rental rooms upstairs in its "lodge," and, in a motel next door, thirteen rooms overlook Silver Lake. The club also has an outdoor beach bar, a pier, and a small beach for swimming. The water is clear, and small fish can be seen swimming near the shore.

Customers range from locals to visitors from as far away as Chicago. One regular "customer" is the club's resident ghost, who is believed to

be Barney Honl. Barney died many years ago in the house next door, but according to Mike and James, he only inhabits the main building. Both James and Mike reported that they have encountered Barney's rather harmless mischief on a regular basis. "People talk of seeing a gentleman in a derby hat and bow tie sitting on the edge of the bed," Mike said. "Pictures on the wall go crooked all at once."

SKY CLUB · *Plover*

A common feature found in many restaurants today got its start as a spark of imagination at Sky Club. Owner Evelyn Schnittger wanted to find a way to keep the assorted dishes of vegetables chilled in the dining room, so customers could make their own salads. She called Russell Swanson, owner of Swanson Equipment Company in nearby Stevens Point. Swanson, whose company was known for building custom bars for taverns all over Wisconsin, became the father of the chilled salad bar, the first of which was installed at the Sky Club in 1951.

The club itself dates back to 1940, when Marion Nall built a home on Highway 51. Next to it, he built a campground, a bar, and a restaurant called Sky Club. The restaurant served sandwiches and baked chicken, and had a couple of gas pumps out front. In 1951, the newly installed all-you-can-eat salad bar became a big draw for the Sky Club.

In 1961, John Freund purchased the restaurant from Evelyn and her husband Louis for $200,000. When John passed away in 1965, his sons Doug, Terrol ("Terry"), and Dennis took over the club. In 1969, the club closed for several months for repairs following a fire. Several additions to the building were made over the years. After Dennis and Terry retired, Terry's sons Eric and Patrick took over the business. And Terry's "retirement" didn't quite take—he headed north, to Boulder Junction, and opened the Headwaters Supper Club. Eric Freund is proud of both his family history and the Sky Club. "Plover exists because of the Sky Club," Eric said. "Our location on Highway 51 was the attraction."

The Sky Club is known for its hand-cut steaks, which are dry-aged for flavor. "I'll put my steak up against Ruth's Chris and blow them out of the water," Eric said. The club also uses local potatoes cultivated on the many potato farms around Plover. Leading the kitchen is head chef Fred Griesbach, one of 20 certified executive chefs in Wisconsin. He has also earned recognition in local, state, and national competitions of the American Culinary Federation.

Right: Owner Eric Freund at the bar.

The menu features steaks and seafood (including the Friday fish fry), plus a variety of combination plates. Many of the fish dishes, as well as appetizers such as the Kermit Legs (frog legs), are fried in a batter made with local Point Amber beer. Another notable dish is the flaming Chateaubriand for two, a large piece of beef tenderloin set afire tableside. Of course, dinner includes a trip to the salad bar. The Sky Club has a large wine list; in fact, one of the club's unofficial mottoes is, "We invite you to wine at the table."

Together, the club's dining rooms and banquet room can seat nearly 500 people. With the exception of the 300-seat banquet room, which is Sky Club's original dining room, each room is separate, offering more intimacy. The main dining room just off the bar area features unique wooden partitions, with brass fixtures and carved wood accents created by Milwaukee architect Walter Neumann. The wood is from the Oshkosh Door Company. "Nobody has a place like this in their hometown. Everyone wants one, but you can't replicate it," Eric said.

Eric plans to stay at the Sky Club for another 20 years to continue "the lost art of dining" that makes supper clubs great. "People come here to eat, drink, socialize; customers expect to see each other. This is their home away from home. It's such a personal service, a tight knit group of bartenders, staff and customers. Like a fraternity."

Below: Jell-o in the salad bar; head chef Fred Griesbach prepares a tray of stuffed pork chops; bags of potatoes.

WASHINGTON INN SUPPER CLUB *Cecil*

ack in 1883, a rail line ran past the front door of the Washington Inn, which served as a boarding house, brothel, and gaming room for the railroad workers. These days, it's best known for the Washington Inn Favorite, a tenderloin stuffed with mozzarella and bacon, and Dar's Special, a deep-fried breaded tenderloin topped with hollandaise and mushrooms. On Mondays and Tuesdays, people line up for the club's broasted chicken or liver and onions specials. The salad bar is included with the meal, and early diners can also enjoy Double Bubble, a two-for-one drink special served from 4 p.m. until 6 p.m., Monday through Saturday.

Current owner Darwin "Dar" Olsen was only 26 when he bought the Washington Inn from Fritz Voecks. Dar began his career in hospitality as a dishwasher at 13. He was cutting steaks at 15, and then went to "chef school," as he put it, ending up as head chef at Dick & Joan's in Appleton.

To get the loan to buy the Washington Inn, Dar leased the restaurant for 11 months to prove to the bank he could run a successful establishment. Sixteen years later, he's still succeeding by keeping his customers happy.

Or at least most of his customers. Dar reported that there is a ghost in the building. The ghost's existence was confirmed by a team of paranormal investigators from Appleton. The ghost is said to be the alcoholic brother of a previous owner. Oddities include drinks that mysteriously disappear, lights that go out in threes, and strange movement of objects around the place.

The
Washington Inn
Supper Club
est. 1883

715.745.2900

Serving You 7 Days a Week
Sunday 10:00am - 9:00pm
Monday -Thursday 4:00pm - 9:00pm
Friday, Saturday 4:00pm -10:00pm

Award Winning Double Bubble
Monday - Saturday 4:00pm - 6:00pm
Sunday 10:00am - 6:00pm

We appreciate your business and hope you enjoy your dining experience today, and always! Thank you!

Your Hosts - Dar, Cari, Jake, Jeric, Abby, & Addy

For all Your Group Gathering Needs: We can accommodate you with a family style dinner or a mini menu. Please advise one of our staff to make arrangements or call 715.745.2900. (Private room charges apply)

Open menu for dinners to go Please call ahead for faster service. A .50 charge will be added to the total per carry-out container.

All prices are subject to sales tax. Not responsible for lost or stolen items during your visit.
A 15% gratuity will be kindly added to parties of 8 or more.

With 187 seats, The Washington Inn is a big place, so the chances of bumping into a drunk ghost are slim. Other, less supernatural leftovers from the club's history are more apparent, though. The Voecks family created the German theme of the exterior; Dar left it, but he believes that it doesn't really apply now. Then there's the "Famous Chicken Dinners" sign, painted in 1940, that still hangs over the door. Dar has left it there for "historic" purposes.

The back of the Washington Inn overlooks Shawano Lake. Sunsets fill the dining room and bar with a warm glow—though some might attribute that to the Double Bubbles.

My Take

When I interviewed Dar, I found him to be a genuinely nice guy with an energetic personality. We also talked about the living space upstairs that served as the original inn, which Dar had converted into an apartment for rent. Having renters above the club turned out to be too much trouble for Dar, so these days, the apartment sits empty.

At the end of our conversation, Dar invited me to sit at the bar for a drink while my dinner was prepared. The bar staff is friendly, and they pour a good drink. Pretty soon, one of the wait staff came over to let me know my table was ready. I tried several items from the salad bar, and then a nice piece of tenderloin with sautéed mushrooms and a breaded walleye filet was set in front of me. Both were excellent, and when Dar came out to ask how the food was, I complimented him on the meal. He seemed truly happy that I had enjoyed his food.

Above: Bartenders Kassidy Hawley, Jasmine Zeuske, and Zachary Sincoular.
Left: Owner Dar Olsen.

WHITE STAG INN *Rhinelander*

The White Stag Inn, at the intersection of State Highway 17 and State Forest Road D, began its days as a tavern called the Laurel Tap. In 1955, a Chicago stonemason named Louie Widule Sr. purchased the tavern and reopened it in 1956 as Louie Widule's White Stag Inn.

A native of Oak Park, Illinois, Louie had designed and installed charcoal broilers for several supper clubs owned by restaurateur George Diamond. When Louie bought the Laurel Tap, he installed two charcoal broilers in the dining room to handle all the cooking. Today, everything at the White Stag Inn is cooked either on the charcoal broilers, right in front of the diners, or in an oven for baking potatoes and rolls. There are no microwaves, fryers, or grease.

Previous page: Co-owner Brian Widule.
Above: Chef Julie Steinmetz prepares the charcoal broiler for some fresh cuts of meat and shrimp.

The menu is simple: eight red-meat options and five fish or chicken options. Meals come with a wedge of iceberg lettuce and the club's home-made salad dressings: Russian cream, French clear, and Caesar. They are made to be enjoyed alone or mixed together. The three dressings are so popular that customers can buy jars of them to take home.

The interior was designed by Louie, who created an appealing mix of meerschaum pipes, mounted deer, works of art, beer steins, and cow skulls. A large painting of tigers hangs behind the bar, painted by Louie's mother in 1902. The elk statue outside, featuring antlers from a real elk, was installed in the early 1990s.

Below: White Stag Inn's three custom salad dressings are available for purchase.

After Louie died, his son David bought the business. David ran the supper club with his wife, Karen, and brother, Louie Jr., before passing the business on to his children: Bradley (Brad), Brian, and Anissa.

A sign out front reads, "If you have reservations, you're in the wrong place." The White Stag Inn may not take reservations, but it is open 361 days a year—a rarity among Wisconsin Northwoods supper clubs. The club closes for just four holidays: Thanksgiving, Christmas Eve, Christmas Day, and Easter.

The White Stag Inn can seat up to 240 guests in its three dining rooms. In the summer months, around 500 meals are served nearly every night. As Brian put it, "In the summer, every night is a Saturday."

Because there are other supper clubs in the area, but no chain restaurants, Brian said the clubs aren't really in competition with one another. "Everyone does something different," he said. "We keep the menu so simple. We cut our own steaks, make our own dressing and baked potato topping. We even make our own old fashioned mix."

Like at many other supper clubs, the staff has stayed much the same for a long time. Waitress Sallie Miller has served suppers for 37 years and bartender Carl Werner has been offering up cocktails for 40 years. Today, the restaurant's experienced hands are passing on their knowledge to a fourth generation of family members—Brad's oldest daughter, Sierra, and her cousin Kathleen—who now work at the White Stag Inn.

Northwest Wisconsin
SUPPER CLUBS

NORTHWEST WISCONSIN IS KNOWN AS INDIAN HEAD COUNTRY because the contour of the western border resembles the profile of a face. The many lakes and hills in this area allow for year-round recreation, which draws lots of visitors, mostly from the Minneapolis-St. Paul area.

Bordered by Lake Superior to the north, this region is also home to the city of Superior, one of the largest ports on the Great Lakes. Just east of Superior is Amnicon Falls State Park; to the south is the National Freshwater Fishing Hall of Fame and Museum, which features a giant statue of a muskellunge (also known as muskie) that's half a block long and over four stories tall.

185

CASTLE HILL SUPPER CLUB *Merrillan*

Castle Hill is located on Highway 12 between Black River Falls and Merrillan, and is neighbor to many Christmas tree farms and one adults-only nudist camp. Castle Hill began as a farmhouse and was later converted into a tavern. In the early 1950s, owners Gert and Harold Johnson transformed the old tavern into the Castle Hill Supper Club and ran it for 25 years. The stories of good food and wild nights that lasted into the wee hours are legendary.

In 1976, Carolyne Hensel and her husband, Bud, of Germantown, Wisconsin, were looking for a change of location and lifestyle, so the couple bought Castle Hill. They were new to the restaurant business, but Gert stayed on for the first six months

Previous page: Owner Carolyne Hensel serves a brandy old-fashioned.

to help them. The eldest Hensel son, Jeff, learned to cook at Castle Hill, and the youngest son, Mike, joined the team in the 1990s. These days, Castle Hill's chef is Carolyne's grandson Nick Tyson, a graduate of the Minneapolis Culinary Arts and Design School.

Bud and Carolyne raised their family in the house next door to the club; to this day the house remains Carolyne's home. Living on site is ideal for commuting, but there are some drawbacks. "Your life is probably not your own," Carolyne said. "Posting the hours on the front doors of the supper club entrance helped, but you get a lot of sales people knocking on your front door at home."

True to its motto, "famous for steaks," Castle Hill serves plenty of tenderloin and prime rib. Just as big a draw, however, is the club's Friday-night seafood buffet, which offers a seemingly endless selection of seafood as well as a few meat offerings. The club also hosts a fish boil, with the cooking done in the kitchen rather than the heavily wooded outdoors.

Each supper served at Castle Hill includes a simple relish tray, bread basket, and soup or salad. The menu is fairly standard supper-club fare, along with some appetizers and sandwiches. "We try to change the menu a bit depending on what people ask for," Carolyne said. The club offers four types of shrimp dinners, as well as a "lite" menu for those who are counting calories.

"We've always had a good reputation for food. We buy the choice or prime beef and try the dishes ourselves," Carolyne said.

Carolyne credits the club's success and longevity to the family-run nature of the business. It ensures that someone who cares is always there to make things right. Some of the customers at Castle Hill have been coming so long that they feel like family too. "We just had a couple celebrate their 53rd anniversary here—they've been customers since 1976," Carolyne said.

DREAMLAND SUPPER CLUB *South Range*

Dreamland's history goes back to 1925, when the Morrison family built it on a plot of land about 10 miles southeast of Superior. Two years later, siblings Fern Gamble and Les Toller bought the property from the Morrisons and took over the club. During Prohibition, the establishment was rumored to be a speakeasy and brothel as well.

In the 1930s, Dreamland featured a Chinese menu. Bands played music from a balcony above the bar, guests danced to the music on a dance floor, and the ceiling was decorated with tinfoil stars. Many years later, the ceiling was lowered to reduce heating costs and the stage above the bar was removed.

Left: Dreamland's relish tray, "bringing the salad bar to your table."

189

In 1956, Betty Brennan bought Dreamland. She sold it to her daughter, Nancy Bergstrom, in 1975; Nancy in turn sold the place to Dan and Terri Patterson in 1999. At the time, Dan was a 20-year veteran of the hospitality industry who had recently earned an MBA.

"What I learned in school was that the restaurant business is tough—don't do it," Dan said. "We had bought a house about a mile away and had never been to supper clubs or Dreamland, but [we] heard it was for sale. Here we are, 13 years later, happy we made the decision."

This page: Crab legs; prime rib.
Next page, from top: Customers Mary Jaques
and Shirley Carroll celebrate a birthday together;
Dreamland's famous French-fried turkey; owner
Dan Patterson makes a cocktail at the bar.

The menu features steaks, seafood, fish, and sandwiches, but the club is best known for its lobsters, which weigh between 16 and 20 ounces. Another popular dish is French-fried turkey, a battered, deep-fried turkey breast served with drawn butter. At Dreamland, the staff likes to call it "the poor man's lobster."

The fried turkey was an invention of Betty Brennan, who passed on the tradition to her granddaughter, who grew up at Dreamland and still occasionally lends a hand.

"There was no written recipe. It was just a little bit of this, a little bit of that," Judy recalled.

Dreamland is open year-round, with many customers arriving on snowmobiles in the winter. The atmosphere is laid back, relaxed, and friendly. Everyone seems to know each other very well, whether they're staff members or customers. Dan runs the bar and seats customers, and Terri works in the kitchen.

"We don't like to rush people because you get so much food here," Terri said. "You get the relish tray, soup, and salad with your meal, plus bread-sticks and crackers—the whole works." In fact, Dan added, some people fill up on the relish tray, soup, and salad, and end up taking their entrées home for later.

Since Dan and Terri have their own home, the upstairs apartment usually remains vacant, save the occasional friend sleeping over. A previous owner swore the place was haunted, but Dan and Terri have never witnessed anything unusual.

FANNIE'S SUPPER CLUB AND MOTEL   *Neillsville*

annie's is located on Highway 10, about six miles
east of Neillsville, amid farms and cow pastures.
Fannie's has had many names over the years, including Steinie's Club 10 and Bali Hai.

Current owners Dan and Merna Elmer bought Fannie's
from Fred and Bernice Barr in 1990. The Elmers had both
worked in the restaurant business for many years—Dan in
the kitchen at Ishnala in Lake Delton, and Merna as a manager at the Hoffman House chain throughout the Midwest.

When Dan and Merna bought Fannie's, the property
included a house next door. They live there to this day, and
they also maintain the 12-unit motel on the west side of the
parking lot. The main dining room overlooks the motel.

"The motel is nice for when we have wedding parties or class reunions. People don't have to worry about driving," Merna said. The large motel rooms are equipped with kitchenettes, including refrigerators and microwaves.

Fannie's bar and main dining room can seat 100, and two large banquet rooms can accommodate another 250. On a busy weekend night, the club serves 150 to 200 dinners.

One of Fannie's most popular dishes is stuffed haddock. "We just sell the heck out of that and the mushroom au gratin appetizer," Merna said. The haddock is filled with crab and bread stuffing, baked in lemon butter, and topped with hollandaise sauce. The mushroom au gratin dish features

193

mushrooms sautéed in butter, mixed with mozzarella cheese, and baked. People often share an order at the bar before sitting down.

In addition to hand-cut steaks and seafood options, Fannie's also offers shrimp de Jonghe and escargots—two items seldom seen on supper club menus north of Beloit.

Fannie's was put up for sale again in 2011. When asked why, Merna said that her kids live in Madison and don't plan to run the club when Dan and Merna retire.

My Take

For this project, I tried to avoid supper clubs that were for sale, so I was surprised to learn after my visit that Fannie's was on the market. However, one supper club owner I talked to said with a laugh, "All supper clubs are for sale, but nobody's buying!"

I spent the night in the motel at Fannie's. I appreciated the spacious room and the fact that I was the only guest there. In the morning, I woke up to a sunny day and some mooing cows across the highway.

As I left the motel and headed west towards Neillsville, I saw a building that looked like an alien spaceship with a 12-foot-tall cow statue standing next to it. It turns out that the "spaceship" is the former site of the 1964 World's Fair's Wisconsin Pavilion. It was shipped back to Wisconsin after the fair, and today it houses the FM rock station WCCN and a gift shop.

The giant cow, called Chatty Belle, is billed as the world's largest talking cow. On that day, however, the talking function was out of order. I was disappointed that I couldn't chat with Miss Belle, but after taking a few photos, I hopped back on the road to my next destination and rocked out to WCCN on the car radio along the way.

HIGH SHORES SUPPER CLUB | *Chippewa Falls*

S ituated on a scenic bluff overlooking Little Lake Wissota, High Shores Supper Club started off as a small bar in 1915, when construction was underway for the hydroelectric dam that would eventually create Big Lake Wissota to the north and Little Lake Wissota to the south. By the 1950s, the original building had been moved across the lake, and in its place a tavern called the Hi-Lo Supper Club was built. Its owners, the Hoover family, sold sandwiches and beer. In the 1960s, the Provoznik family renamed it the High Shores Haus, and changed the menu to reflect a German influence. In the 1970s, the Provozniks sold the club to the Piller family, who ran it for a few years.

The building was vacant when current owners Denny and Diane Schroeder took ownership in 1994. They changed the club's name to the High Shores Supper Club, redecorated the interior

with musical instruments, and later added the log exterior. Denny, Diane, and their three daughters lived in the apartment below the club for three years before buying a nearby house. Today, they occasionally rent out the apartment.

The High Shores was Denny's first experience running a restaurant. On the night the club opened, Denny hid the money from the cash register in the family's dishwasher. Unfortunately, he didn't realize that the dishwasher worked. Later, he found that the money had been thoroughly washed, so he spent a fair amount of time drying them out with with a hair dryer. As Denny put it, "My first night in the business, I was laundering money!"

Left: Owners Denny and Diane Schroeder.
Above: Violins on display as part of the musical instrument motif.

Besides amazing views of the lake, High Shores offers a unique blend of traditional supper club fare. Favorites include Black Angus prime rib, a 16-ounce tenderloin, and seafood. The club also offers specials, such as Alaskan creamy parmesan whitefish, citrus salsa Cajun salmon, and one item that is as unusual as it is popular—alligator, served Cajun style and deep fried or broiled. Flatbread pizzas and pasta dishes are also on the menu, and supper includes a 50-item soup and salad bar.

Previous page: Denny Schroeder shows
off a Canadian walleye pike filet.
This page: Baked cod; Cajun alligator
appetizer; the pink squirrel, an after-
dinner ice cream drink.

Little Lake Wissota offers year-round recreation. In the summer months, High Shores offers a champagne boat cruise that includes a 90-minute trip around the lake. Guests can see legendary beer brewer Jacob Leinenkugel's house and hear the story of how the lake was formed, and then enjoy a full dinner back on shore.

The dining room seats about 110, and in warmer months, guests can also eat on the outdoor patio, which seats almost 150. On a busy Friday, 250 to 300 diners enjoy the fish fry. The boat dock can accommodate quite a few boats, but Denny warned, "There are times when the boats will line up and wait to get a space."

Diane is proud of the warm and welcoming atmosphere she's established, and she enjoys greeting newcomers as well as regulars. Several years ago, Led Zeppelin singer Robert Plant paid

Above: Diane Schroeder chats with customers at the bar. Next page: Waitress Jennifer See shows off the dessert items.

a visit to the club; after playing at the nearby Cadott Rock Festival, he stopped by for a catfish dinner. Diane wasn't too sure who he was, but Denny recognized him. Both found him to be relaxed and friendly.

When asked if any of their daughters were interested in taking over the business, Diane said, "They're grown up and married. They saw what we did here and thought, 'Mom and Dad work too hard!'"

INDIANHEAD SUPPER CLUB | *Balsam Lake*

The Indianhead Supper Club looks much the same as when it opened as the Indianhead Lodge in 1939. Seated on a bluff overlooking Mill Pond Lake, the club is a destination for local residents and visitors from as far away as Minneapolis. The ambience is that of a warm and cozy log cabin adorned with black velvet paintings of Native Americans. As the Indianhead fills up for the night, a piano player sits near the entrance, entertaining diners and those waiting for a table.

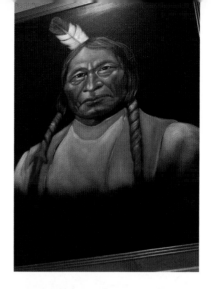

The heart of the Indianhead is its kitchen, helmed by head chef Roark Flenniken and sous chef Jay Gisvold. Chef Roark has run the kitchen for the past seven years, and Jay has been at his side at the Indianhead for two, but the pair have worked together on and off in various kitchens for twenty-five years. They're best friends, and it shows in the quiet symmetry they share in the tiny kitchen as they turn out dish after dish for a busy dining room.

Below: Chef Roark Flenniken (center) visits with longtime customers Lynne and Jack MacBean.

"We do what we want," Roark said. "You can sell really good food in the middle of nowhere."

Customers Lynne and Jack MacBean dine at Indianhead once a week. Jack even has his own bobblehead doll, which is placed on their table when they dine.

"This place has better food than any place in Minneapolis," Lynne said.

Jack raved about the club's filet. "I'd put them up against Ruth's Chris or Morton's any day," he said.

Because Lynne is such a cherished regular, Roark prepares a special dish for her: a filet of salmon in puff pastry. It occasionally appears as a special on the menu, but he makes it any time Lynne is there, and she loves it.

Chef Roark makes BBQ ribs in a smoker on the side of the kitchen. He cooks eight full racks, and and "when they're gone, they're gone," as he put it.

Indianhead features theme nights as well, including Greek and Mexican nights and a Hawaiian luau feast, each of which includes a five-course dinner with wine pairings.

From top: Filet of salmon in puff pastry; chicken piccata; pineapple upside-down cake. Next page: An old menu advertises steak sandwiches for one dollar and tea for ten cents; racks of ribs; balsam burger with bacon and cheese.

Welcome To

INDIAN HEAD LODGE

BALSAM LAKE, WISCONSIN

We Specialize In

Steaks   Chicken

Barbecued Ribs and Beef

Seafoods

ALSO

The Best of Liquors

Special Accommodations for Parties

PHONE 2416   JACK AND ALYCE FERGUSON, PR

MENU

TWO PORK CHOPS	$1.65
TENDERLOIN STEAKS	$2.50
EXTRA SPECIAL T-BONE STEAKS	$3.00
SIRLOIN STEAKS	$3.00
BARBECUED BEEF	$1.65
BARBECUED RIBS	$1.65
FROG LEGS	$1.65
BROOK TROUT	$1.65
FRENCH FRIED SHRIMP	$1.65
LOBSTER TAILS	$2.25
FRIED PIKE FILLET	$1.65
½ FRIED CHICKEN	$1.75
SPECIAL T-BONE	$2.50

Above orders include French fried potatoes, salad, relish, bread, butter, beverage and dessert.

SANDWICHES

BARBECUE BEEF	$ .45
HAM	$ .45
BACON, LETTUCE & TOMATO	$ .45
GRILLED CHEESE	$ .45
STEAK	$1.00
PORK CHOP	$1.00
HAMBURGER	$ .45

Pork chops and steak sandwich includes French frys, salad, and beverage.

ALA CARTE ORDERS

SHRIMP COCKTAIL	$ .75
CHILI CON CARNE	$ .25
BOWL FRENCH FRIES	$ .25
COFFEE ....$ .10 TEA ....$ .10 MILK ....$ .10	

Below: Crab cakes with pesto aioli; shrimp lollipops; prime rib; scallops with saffron-flavored ravioli. Next page, from top: Cedar-plank walleye and cedar-plank salmon; a pianist entertains guests; sous chef Jay Gisvold and head chef Roark Flenniken in the kitchen.

My Take

After arriving at the Indianhead, I went into the kitchen to take a few photos of food coming off the line. Suddenly Roark was sending over dishes for me to try: tender crab cakes with pesto aioli, full of crab meat and perfectly cooked; as well as shrimp "lollipops," skewered jumbo shrimp with Thai curry paste, fried in a wonton shell. Then there was the topper: grilled scallops with saffron-flavored pasta, stuffed with spinach and cheese and served on a bed of mixed leeks and assorted mushrooms. It was one of the most flavorful and unique dishes that I've ever had. I was honored to be the recipient to such a grand meal—in the chef's kitchen, no less.

I asked to take a photo of Jay and Roark, but it took some coaxing to get Roark to smile. I soon found that when Roark talks about food, his face lights up. He loves to talk about cooking and enjoys seeing the reaction of someone savoring a dish he made.

Hot pan!

THE LAUREL   *New Richmond*

Roberta and Glen Little have owned the Laurel Supper Club, located seven miles east of New Richmond on State Trunk Highway 64, since 2005. They purchased the club from Gary Gorka, who had owned it since 1990.

Head chef Gus Gusa has presided over the kitchen since 2004, following 23 years at Southview Country Club in West St. Paul, Minnesota. He happened to stop in for a drink one day—the same day Gary happened to be looking for a chef.

The Laurel is best known for its steaks and popovers. When asked about the popularity of popovers in northwestern Wisconsin, Gus said, "It's a Norwegian thing." The popovers at the Laurel are served with a side of honey butter at the start of every meal. The club serves such entrées as a steak dinner for two, which is soup, salad, popovers, a 24-ounce top sirloin, and a bottle of wine or champagne.

Left: Hot popovers served with honey butter.
Below left: Oscar the buck and his antlers.

The Laurel, which is open seven days a week, is small but has two floors. The ground-floor dining room seats 75, plus another 20 fit at the bar. The downstairs banquet room and bar will seat another 120.

The mounted deer head on the wall once belonged to a deer named Oscar, who lived in captivity behind the Laurel for almost 25 years. Twelve racks of his antlers are also on display, along with a few foxes.

PINE RIDGE | Stone Lake

Surrounded by a dense cover of pine trees, the Pine Ridge Supper Club is part of a cluster of houses and condominiums on the northern shoreline of Sissabagama Lake, about 20 miles south of Hayward.

The building, which was used as a fishing cabin in the late 19th century, was converted into a tavern and lodge in 1920. Today, the tavern lives on as Pine Ridge's front bar. Over the years, a total of fourteen cabins were built on the surrounding property, and in the 1970s, then-owners Ken and Sandy Knutson added a dining room and living quarters. Finally, in the 1980s, the surrounding cabins were sold off as condominiums.

Current owner Mike Snyder bought Pine Ridge in 1996, after he had spent nearly two decades working at a restaurant called Michael's in Rockford, Illinois. Mike had always wanted to run his own restaurant, and he believed that running one in the Hayward area (near a cabin owned by his father) would be more feasible than opening a restaurant in a city.

The Pine Ridge had been closed for a few years and was in need of improvements, but Mike managed to reopen the restaurant within a month of buying it. "People on the lake were excited that I was opening, but I wanted to go slowly, without big crowds, so expectations weren't too high," Mike said. "Although the first night was a fish fry, and we were pretty busy."

On Fridays, the menu is limited to the fish fry and broasted chicken. On those nights, 500 dinners are generally served, so the club simply couldn't get the food out fast enough if it offered a full menu. Even still, on Fridays people wait two hours or longer for a table, sometimes tailgating outside while they wait—something the neighbors aren't always happy about.

"I'm more of a restaurant than a bar," Mike added. "Most Fridays, we're closed by 11 p.m."

One offering unique to the Pine Ridge is its fry bread, which is served with every meal. This traditional Native American dish was on the menu when Mike bought the club, and he has continued it in his own way. Mike serves six pieces in a basket, topped with powdered sugar, resulting in a snack that looks a bit like a doughnut. Fry bread is normally cooked in lard, but Mike switched to vegetable oil because the lard got too messy. Aside from the fish fry, fry bread is the club's most popular item. "People love that fry bread!" Mike said.

Clockwise from top: cooking up fry bread; Pine Ridge fish fry; fry bread served in a basket with powdered sugar.

Mike, his wife Kathy, and his daughters Amanda and Lisa have lived in the apartment above the club since it opened. He loves the business, but has mixed feelings about living above the supper club. He wishes there was more space for the kids to play.

Still, he likes the fact that there are no nearby chain restaurants to compete with. "I go to the other supper clubs," Mike said. "They're not enemies or competitors. They are my friends."

213

THE RANCH · *Hayward*

uilt by John and Marie Anderson in
1930 as the Aladdin, the Ranch was
originally billed as Hayward's Smart
Nite Club. It featured a tavern and
dance hall on what was then the outskirts of
town. Legend has it that FBI agents sometimes
posed as busboys in the tavern in an attempt
to catch various mobsters and criminals when
they visited the club.

In 1959, a legendary local character, Vivian
Levinson, bought the club. She renamed it the
Ranch in honor of her collection of wild deer, buf-
falo, and other animals housed behind the club.

Next page: Steak with mushrooms and sautéed
shrimp and scallops; owners (from left) Beth Morgan,
Barnaby Morgan, and Cheryl Haupt behind the bar.

Sometimes, one of Vivian's buffalo would wander off into town and would need to be rounded up and sent back to the Ranch.

John and Janet Buege bought the Ranch in 1979, and in 1987, they sold it to sisters Cheryl Haupt and Beth Morgan and their respective husbands, Peter and Barnaby. Today, Cheryl, Beth, and Barnaby are co-owners.

Cheryl and Beth, who were working at the club when they bought it, still work the front of the house, while Barnaby mans the kitchen. Some of Barnaby's specialties include walleye scampi and walleye-and-wild-rice fish cake, which is similar to a crab cake.

The menu at the Ranch is fairly simple, covering the basics—along with a few specials. "Being up here, you can't get too complicated with the menu. You can tell when the vacation people are here—they order the specials," Barnaby said.

215

The club can serve 125 to 135 dinners on a busy Saturday, with seating for 50 to 60 in the main dining area and 40 more in a side room.

"You're nothing without repeat customers, and our business is built on that," Beth said. "We're familiar, friendly, and consistent." Some customers are so regular, she added, that tables are unofficially named after them.

When asked about the average age of their customers, Cheryl joked, "We've always got an ambulance idling out front."

Above: Cheryl Haupt, Beth Morgan, Jim Duffy, Barnaby Morgan, Barbara Duffy, Jan Anderson, and Rick Anderson chat at the bar.

THE STEAK PIT *Washburn*

This popular supper club began in 1973, when Edie and John Deutsch bought the Swan Supper Club and renamed it the Steak Pit. In 1982, the couple moved the club from Washburn's main drag, Bayfield Street, to a new home beside Lake Superior's Vandeventer Bay, which had a brand-new marina.

John had worked as a chef at a popular hotel in Superior, Wisconsin, before meeting Edie and opening the Steak Pit. They don't quite remember where the name came from, though Edie thinks it might have been a variation on a submission to a newspaper contest.

Edie's take on the restaurant's success is simple. "All I know is you've got to work and work hard, run a first-class place, and try to be better than the other ones," she said.

The club serves fresh, locally sourced lake trout, and fish. As Edie's son Bob put it, "Caught today, served today." The Steak Pit also features local dairy products, including homemade ice cream. Soups, dressings, and salads are also made from scratch in the club's spacious kitchen.

Edie leaves the day-to-day operations to her sons, Jim and Bob, and her stepson Jerry is the manager—but she keeps an eye on them. All three men are proud of the club's long history, noting that other supper clubs have changed hands frequently.

Above: James Thoreson with hand-breaded onion rings ready for frying. Next page: Edie Deutsch with her stepson, Jerry Sukala, and son, James Thoreson.

The Steak Pit's back bar has a longer history than the restaurant itself. It was one of two built for the 1933 Chicago World's Fair by the Brunswick Balke Collender Company of Germany.

John's nephew created the giant T-bone steak sign over the entrance and drove it nearly 300 miles from Battle Lake, Minnesota, to Washburn. A Florida artist named Fishbone crafted the metal artwork on the club's walls and room dividers, which are reminiscent of the Ashland shoreline. Jerry hired Fishbone to create the art after seeing his work in a Florida restaurant. While Fishbone was in town installing the pieces, he gave art lessons to locals.

With such a big dining room, the Steak Pit can serve 200 to 300 meals on summer nights. The club is open seven days a week, which is unusual in northern Wisconsin. "People get tired of places that change their hours or days they're open," Jerry said. "They always know we're open. It gets kind of tough in the winter, but we manage."

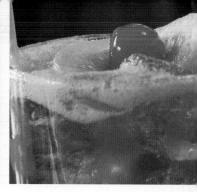

Making an Old-Fashioned

The aptly-named old-fashioned was created long before Prohibition. Originally just whiskey, bitters, and sugar, it has undergone many iterations throughout its tenure as a standard cocktail. In Wisconsin, where the old-fashioned is the unofficial state drink, the overwhelming preference is to serve it with brandy instead of whiskey.

Recipe

HAND-MUDDLED BRANDY OLD-FASHIONED SWEET

1 maraschino cherry
1/2 slice of orange
1 sugar cube or 1 t sugar
2–3 dashes of bitters
1 1/2–2 oz brandy
7UP
ice

In a 10- or 12-ounce tumbler, combine the cherry, orange, sugar, and bitters. Muddle (mash) together.

Add ice, then the brandy, and top off with 7UP. Garnish with an orange slice and a maraschino cherry.

Non-muddled brandy old-fashioneds are made with sugar or simple syrup (sugar dissolved in water), bitters, and 7UP, or with a ready-made old-fashioned mix. In addition to the orange and cherry, garnishes sometimes include green olives stuffed with pimentos or bleu cheese, marinated mushrooms, pickled asparagus, or a wedge of pineapple.

A brandy old-fashioned can also be ordered sour (using sour mix or lemonade), press (using half 7UP, half soda water) and soda (using carbonated water).

Supper Club Sources

SOUTHEAST WISCONSIN

THE COPPER DOCK
1474 E. Friess Lake Drive
Hubertus, WI 53033
(262) 628-3718
www.foodspot.com/Clients/WI/
Hubertus/CopperDockRestaurant/
default.aspx?accid=20057

DIAMOND JIM'S STONERIDGE INN
11811 W. Janesville Road
Hales Corners, WI 53130
(414) 425-7777
www.diamondjimsstoneridgeinn.com

THE DUCK INN
N6214 Wisconsin 89
Delavan, WI 53115
(608) 883-6988
www.duckinndelavan.com

ELIAS INN SUPPER CLUB
200 N. 2nd Street
Watertown, WI 53094
(920) 261-6262

HOBNOB
277 S. Sheridan Road
Racine, WI 53403
(262) 552-8008
www.thehobnob.com

JACKSON GRILL
3736 W. Mitchell Street
Milwaukee, WI 53215
(414) 384-7384
www.thejacksongrill.com

SOUTHWEST WISCONSIN

3 MILE HOUSE
370 State Road 35
Hazel Green, WI 53811
(680) 748-4455
www.3milehousedining.com

BENEDETTI'S SUPPER CLUB
3232 Riverside Drive
Beloit, WI 53511
(608) 362-9917
www.benedettisclub51.wordpress.com

BUCKHORN SUPPER CLUB
11802 N. Charley Bluff Road
Milton, WI 53563
(608) 868-2653
www.thebuckhorn.net

THE BUTTERFLY CLUB
5246 E. City Road X
Beloit, WI 53511
(608) 362-8577
www.butterflyclub.us

CIMAROLI'S SUPPER CLUB
W11793 State Road 127
Portage, WI 53901
(608) 742-2238
www.cimarolis.com

**COUNTRY HEIGHTS SUPPER
CLUB AND MOTEL**
1154 Badger Road
Hazel Green, WI 53811
(608) 748-4687
www.countryheightssupperclub
andmotel.com

DING-A-LING SUPPER CLUB
8215 W. Race Street
Hanover, WI 53542
(608) 879-9209
www.ding-a-lingsupperclub.com

DORF HAUS
8931 County Road Y
Sauk City, WI 53583
(608) 643-3980
www.foodspot.com/Clients/WI/
SaukCity/DorfHausSupperClub/
default.aspx?accid=19510

ISHNALA
S2011 Ishnala Road
Lake Delton, WI 53940
(608) 253-1771
www.ishnala.com

JONES' BLACK ANGUS
37640 US 18
Prairie du Chien, WI 53821
(608) 326-2222

LIBERTY INN
1901 E. Liberty Avenue
Beloit, WI 53511
(608) 362-2262
www.singlestopmarketing.com/
libertyinn-beloit

ROCKY'S SUPPER CLUB
101 S. Main Street—Highway 35
Stoddard, WI 54658
(608) 457-2111
www.rockysrestaurant.com

SMOKY'S
3005 University Avenue
Madison, WI 53705
(608) 233-2120
www.smokysclub.com

SULLIVAN'S SUPPER CLUB
W25709 Sullivan Road
Trempealeau, WI 54661
(608) 534-7775
www.sullivanssupperclub.com

TORNADO STEAK HOUSE
116 S. Hamilton Street
Madison, WI 53703
(608) 256-3570
www.tornadosteakhouse.com

NORTHEAST WISCONSIN

KROPP'S SUPPER CLUB
4570 Shawno Avenue
Green Bay, WI 54313
(920) 865-7331
www.kroppssupperclub.com

LOX CLUB
591 State Street—County Highway Z
Combined Locks, WI 54113
(920) 788-4401
www.witowns.com/LoxClubHome.htm

THE MILL SUPPER CLUB
4128 Wisconsin 42
Sturgeon Bay, WI 54235
(920) 743-5044
www.millsupperclub.com

PRIME STEER SUPPER CLUB
704 Hyland Avenue
Kaukauna, WI 54130
(920) 766-9888
www.primesteersupperclub.com

ROEPKE'S VILLAGE INN
W2686 Saint Charles Road
Chilton, WI 53014
(920) 849-4000
www.roepkesvillageinn.com

SCHWARZ'S SUPPER CLUB
W1688 Sheboygan Road
New Holstein, WI 53061
(920) 894-3598
www.schwarzsupperclub.com

SHAFFER PARK RESORT AND SUPPER Club
N7217 Shaffer Road
Crivitz, WI 54114
(715) 854-2184
www.shafferparkresort.com

SUNSET SUPPER CLUB
N7364 Winnebago Drive
Fond du Lac, WI 54935
(920) 922-4540
www.sunsetsupperclub.com

NORTH CENTRAL WISCONSIN

ANTLERS SUPPER CLUB
120 E. Green Bay Street
Bonduel, WI 54107
(715) 758-2190

BERNARD'S COUNTRY INN
701 2nd Street N.
Stevens Point, WI 54481
(715) 344-3365
www.bernardscountryinn.com

BUCK-A-NEER SUPPER CLUB
D1891 County Road C
Stratford, WI 54484
(715) 384-2629
www.marshfieldrestaurants.com/
buckaneer.html

MAIDEN LAKE SUPPER CLUB
15649 Maiden Lake Road
Mountain, WI 54149
(715) 276-6479
www.maidenlakesupperclub.com/
contact.html

MAMA'S SUPPER CLUB
10486 Highway 70 W.
Minocqua, WI 54548
(715) 356-5070
www.mamassupperclub.com

MARTY'S PLACE NORTH
2721 US Highway 51 N.
Arbor Vitae, WI 54568
(715) 356-4335
www.martysplacenorth.com

NORWOOD PINES SUPPER CLUB
10171 Highway 70
Minocqua, WI 54548
(715) 356-3666
www.norwoodpines.com

PINEWOOD SUPPER CLUB
1208 Halfmoon Lake Drive
Mosinee, WI 54455
(715) 693-3180
www.thepinewood.com

THE SILVERCRYST
W7015 Highway 21 East
Wautoma, WI 54982
(800) 358-9663
www.silvercryst.com

SKY CLUB
2200 Post Road
Plover, WI 54467
(715) 341-4000
www.skyclubdining.com

WASHINGTON INN SUPPER CLUB
101 S. Warrington Street
Cecil, WI 54166
(715) 745-2900
www.theinn.boparound.com

WHITE STAG INN
7141 Wisconsin 17
Rhinelander, WI 54501
(715) 272-1057

NORTHWEST WISCONSIN

CASTLE HILL SUPPER CLUB
N9581 US Highway 12
Merrillan, WI 54754
(715) 333-5901
www.castlehillsupperclub.com

DREAMLAND SUPPER CLUB
4368 S. City Road East
South Range, WI 54874
(715) 398-3706
www.dreamlandsupperclub.com

FANNIE'S SUPPER CLUB AND MOTEL
W3741 US Highway 10
Neillsville, WI 54456
(715) 743-2169
www.fanniessupperclubandmotel.com

HIGH SHORES SUPPER CLUB
17985 County Highway X
Chippewa Falls, WI 54729
(715) 723-9854
www.highshores.com

INDIANHEAD SUPPER CLUB
107 Indianhead Shores Drive
Balsam Lake, WI 54810
(715) 485-3359
www.indianheadsupperclub.com

THE LAUREL
1905 State Trunk Highway 64
New Richmond, WI 54017
(715) 246-5121

PINE RIDGE
16618 W. Sissabagama Road
Stone Lake, WI 54876
(715) 865-2796
www.pineridgewi.com

THE RANCH
10590 N. Ranch Road
Hayward, WI 54843
(715) 634-2090
www.haywardsoriginalsteakhouse.com

THE STEAK PIT
125 Harbor View Drive
Washburn, WI 54891
(715) 373-5492
www.steakpit.net

ACKNOWLEDGMENTS

My HEARTFELT THANKS go out to the following friends and family members who have helped make this book possible:

Charlene and Oswald Lettrari, Ron Faiola Sr., Eric Melger, and Tracy Mielcarek-Melger for their support and assistance, especially while I was on the road.

Rick Kogan for being the spark that got this book going, Thomas Dvorak for helping me with NETA and PBS, Garry Denny for his support, and Michael Bowen for his helpful advice.

Special thanks go to Tim and Denise Dodge, Tony and Vicki Kunz, Rich and Kimberly Lock, Katy and Jim Young, Joe Hausch, Mike Mellock, Erik and Sara Heggland, and Andrew Ottinger.

And finally, a tip o' the hat and a hearty handclasp to the folks who gave me some great supper club recommendations, both in person and via social media.

ABOUT THE AUTHOR

Ron Faiola got his start in the food service industry as a teenager, when he worked in the kitchen of a Kentucky Fried Chicken. Later, he became a short order cook at a greasy spoon and then paid his way through film school at University of Wisconsin–Milwaukee by making sub sandwiches. The subject of his first student film was cocktail wieners (*Wieners*, 1987).

Faiola was a video specialist for a Milwaukee law firm before starting his own production company, Push Button Gadget, Inc. In 2009, Faiola produced and directed *Fish Fry Night Milwaukee*, a documentary about the popular Wisconsin tradition of Friday night fish fry. His follow-up, *Wisconsin Supper Clubs: An Old Fashioned Experience* (2011), showcased the unique locations, food, and atmosphere of 14 supper clubs around the state. *Wisconsin Supper Clubs* has appeared on PBS stations nationwide and earned mentions in such newspapers as the *New York Times*, *Chicago Tribune*, *Washington Post*, and *Milwaukee Journal Sentinel*, as well as other print and web-based media around the US.